From Golem to Mormon

Or

A Physical and Spiritual Survival Story

By Corie Richter

Dedicated to those who went far in pushing forward the work started by the Lord:

Cathy

Ginger

Harold

Lee

Linda

Lisa

Luckie

Myron

Roger

And a special thanks to the former Utah bishop who set it all right, renewing a neophyte's faith in the church. You know who you are ☺

TABLE OF CONTENTS

Preface

The title of this book may come as a curiosity to some. **Golem,** in Hebrew, means something that is incomplete. According to a widespread Jewish lore, it is without shape, injected with life by magic to serve its creator. In many ways that was me: but I do not think it ever occurred to me I was serving my creator. Yes, I did a lot of volunteer work when young, served my country, saved a few lives along the way, and comforted terminal patients, including AIDS victims. I was not a stellar human being; but many were much worse and that is how I judged myself. Not exactly reaching for divine approval.

In many ways, becoming a member of the Church of Jesus Christ of Latter-day Saints was the antithesis of what beliefs I held. My friends see a difference in me that I do not. However, I know I look at life from another vantage point. Without doubt, it was a life (and eternal) alteration in direction. I am grateful for it: but it did not come easily.

Why write the book and why you might want to read it?

If you are looking for Mormon-bashing, look elsewhere.

It is about Mormons and how a single, older woman, born of Jewish parents, learned to survive conversion and culture.

It is not a "happy, happy" book where everyone is perfect and caring. This is about reality.

The descriptions of events sometimes point to local leadership along this journey, not exactly exerting their authority appropriately. It is **not** a condemnation of the hierarchy or doctrine

There are 2 take-home lessons. The first being that we can always find excuses to drop out (the preferred euphemism is "become less active"): but that is foolish. There is a reward for enduring to the end. The second of these lessons is that culture is not doctrine: though I have found many good and faithful saints do not particularly "get it".

Why not publish through a "regular" publishing house? There are publishers who jump on anything that can be perceived as negative about the LDS church, or Christianity in general. I have no intention of feeding that frenzy. Traditional LDS publishers prefer books that are devoid of less than admirable actions of members and leaders; unless, I suspect, there is a lesson in repentance. I want people to read the book to gain or strengthen their testimonies, as they walk down the road of my trials. It is not for a vacation fund in Pango Pango, Mozambique or to enhance the coffers of a publishing house who thinks we are a cult. In short, it is not about money.

It is not the church that causes the problems: it is the people. You will find it in every religion, bar none.

President Brigham Young (1801–77**),** "*The most effectual way to establish the religion of Heaven is to live it, rather than to die for it: I think I am safe in saying that there are many of the Latter-day Saints who are more willing to die for their religion than to live it faithfully*" (Discourses of Brigham Young, sel. John A. Widtsoe [1954], 221).

Chasing the Dead

About the time Joseph was organizing the Church of Jesus Christ of Latter-day Saints, my great-great grandfather and his family were joyfully celebrating their love of and devotion to their God. This was in spite of the frequent raids of genocide, beatings, burnings, debilitating taxes and out-rights cruelty towards the Jewish community; in the Ukraine. He was, you see, a member of a relatively new and then obscure movement called Breslov Chassiduth (Hassidism). The religious zealots practiced an orthodox form of Judaism that was born in Eastern Europe. I think the most succinct description comes from a 19th century sage, Rabbi Sholom DovBer Schneersohn (1860-1920): *"A Hassid is a lamplighter"*. This particular brand of worship stressed daily prayer; but also communicating with God in one's own words. Though it has undergone something of an extremist metamorphosis in the past two hundred years, the original intent was to do away with the "elite", to bring the Lord into the hearts and minds of the common man, and to live righteously in anticipation of the coming Messiah. They were tired of the "letter of the law" as opposed to the intent.

Well, yes, they missed the boat on the Messiah; but their hearts were otherwise in the right place. My urZaide (great grandfather) was a lay teacher of the holy writ. His daughter married and immigrated to the United States at the beginning of the 20th century. In that society we can rest assured no father would let someone other than a like-minded righteous man marry into the family. Unfortunately, we know little of my grandfather, other than he served his country (Ukraine, Prussian or Russia) as a soldier. This information comes from a lost photograph that was copied and oil painted many years ago. Logic would dictate he came from a town not far from Uman, where my grandmother lived. They were married before they left the Ukraine. We know he changed his name, as did his brothers who preceded him; and no one remains who knows what their original surname was.

What little knowledge I have is that Grandmother crossed the veil at the age of 30: leaving behind 2 children under the age of 6. I have to assume my grandfather, who I remember as a steel-hard man with no humor or empathy, likely lost his faith and emotions with her death. He remarried within a year to a widow, and ultimately raised their 4 children. His two original sons were raised without any love or religion in their lives, though they lived the culture. Neither received a bar mitzvah: the holy ceremony of manhood in the religion. Their half-brother did, plus a college education. The story reads like a classic Cinderella

9

without a fairy god-mother, and they were damaged merchandise. Each had dropped out of school by the age of 16. They married sisters (literally 2 brothers married to 2 sisters) and raised their children because it was expected: not because they wanted children or to change the path of their lives.

I was brought to the church: of this there is no doubt. It was not until I learned the existence and purpose of temples that I began to comprehend why. It never occurred to me it was Heavenly Father's inexplicable love for me as well as my devoted progenitors.

I am convinced my grandmother and great grandparents accepted the gospel even before I took on this mortality. They were waiting for me: a rebellious and uncompromising offspring who challenged everything that most people took for granted. I can honestly say that the way my life was going, there was very little chance I would come through for them: but they and the Lord made it happen. Coming to the church was only the first step. I did not join until I was past 60; and my mother was in her 80's with a not-so-accurate memory of things she once knew. My father never shared anything with us about his real mother: in fact, I was 18 before learning the witch who I knew as my grandmother, was not. My father died at 50.

How I found clues is another story: but the Lord deserves the credit, not me.

The late 1800's pogroms, Russian revolution, and rise of the Soviet Union effectively wiped out most Jewish communities if not records, in that area of the world. What was left of them in the Ukraine after WWII was little. However, even after the fall of the communist state, the Ukrainians destroyed remnants of most Jewish cemeteries: many that were hundreds of years old. They built housing projects and even a State television station over them, including one that was a memorial to 17,000 Jews killed, in Kiev. The Lord's work will never stop; but some things may have to wait for the millennium to be sorted out.

I can tell you I did not come to the church on a whim or to experiment. No missionaries were involved, and I did not spend sleepless nights wondering whether the church is true. I will simply say that I am here to tell you it is where the Lord wants me. Was it a reward for my faithful ancestors? I have no doubt that was: but part of it. However, I am evidence of the Gathering and the Lord's hand.

From There to Here

We should probably start with my roots. It is likely only unusual if you grew up in a righteous home.

My father was a bad businessman with a massive ego. Money was a driving force, and he was rarely good at earning it in the quantities he yearned. He practiced the brand of morality where the end justified the means: any action was fair game as long as you were not caught. He went to the synagogue on the high holidays, sometimes fasted on Yom Kippur (the day of atonement), and considered himself forgiven for the next year: when he would repeat the very same acts, only to again spend one day a year going through the ritualistic fast. It is about here that some of you are likely thinking about the stereotypical Jewish community. Don't. People of all religions are a product of their family's environment. Those who are raised without love and without a true knowledge of God's works are incomplete and know no better in what the Lord expects. Someone who actually KNOWS the teachings and breaks the commandments is responsible: but the Lord has told us he will not hold those who do not know, accountable. Something else to consider: frequently, in the Gospel Doctrine class I lead, we discuss our responsibility to point out or butt out when unrighteousness is observed. I am not here to go into a soliloquy on that, but will relate an incident that you can ponder.

Years after my father died, I had a conversation with my father's brother, who I stopped to see on a Florida business trip. The old man had something on his mind and wanted to talk. He nearly broke down into tears when he told me how sorry he was that he did not intervene, though knowing my father had beat me on a regular basis. It was easier, he said, to keep quiet rather than incur his brother's wrath and damage their relationship. What do you say to a frail elderly man with remorse? So long after the fact it made little difference; so I just told him it was okay.

The saddest part of my father's actions, or inactions, is how it impacted his children. Though I was the only one who incurred his physical and mental abuse, my siblings have a different view of ethics and morality than I. We did not grow up in the righteous household of any religion. I, by no means, was an exemplar of virtue: but I always have marched to the tune of a different drummer.

They shipped me off to learn Hebrew when I was around 8 years old. That torture became a two-way street. They could answer no questions: and I had plenty of them. It did not endear me to them or draw us closer when they skirted the issue. A bonus was the incredible dislike my teacher demonstrated. That was okay with me: I had no love for him either. It made no sense to me to learn to read a new language I did not understand. Neither one of my parents could read it either (though it took me years to realize that because they would never admit not knowing anything); but they could not be out-done by neighbors and friends. They belonged to conservative synagogues as I grew up, and mocked the reformed movement. Odd, since that was where congregants actually understood what they were reading because it was in English.

In the first year of elementary school I grew curious about Christians, Christmas and where Santa fit into this equation. I wanted to know what and who they were, plus why I went to all the parties but we did not have one or a tree. I was equally concerned as to why my mother dragged me to see Santa yearly to have my picture taken with him. He always asked me whether I was good and what I wanted for the holiday we did not celebrate. I was the only one in my class who was not visited by the mysterious man. It never occurred to me to ask before I went to school, because I had no friends prior to starting my school days. I remember the day we returned from Christmas break. When I got home, I asked my mother. Even at that age, I had doubts she was telling the truth when she mumbled something that made no sense. Her explanation of Jesus Christ was, even to my naïve ears, something absurd. She lost her credibility all together the next day when I asked the same to an Italian friend. After all, who would know better than the class leader in demerits but who had a room full of new toys? He not so patiently explained what a first-grader might know. At that moment I realized what I was hearing was closer to the truth than the stupid answer given by the woman I was supposed to trust. There is a lesson in that for parents who want to retain a confident relationship with their kids.

We moved before I entered high school, to upstate New York. The intellectual discourse on religion was a step above what I had in elementary school. Much to my parents' consternation, most of my friends were not Jewish. I studied Judaism, under duress, through those years, though I always thought there was something missing. I was determined that I would, one day, find out what that was.

When it was time for college, I went as far away as I could; landing in Iowa. It was a defining moment for me not only because I escaped the clutches of a physically and emotionally abusive household, but because at the Quaker school I was introduced to the scriptures. I have never qualified as scriptoria, but I did slog my way through with startling good grades. I often think most of my basic biblical education came by means of osmosis. The class was held early in the morning (9 A.M.), way before I wanted to arise. I would sit in the back row, wear my sunglasses, and rest my head against the wall to keep from nodding when I slept. In retrospect, perhaps there was a divine reason I came to that school and became ingrained with the sacred text. I cannot say I took it seriously, but knew there were lessons to be learned. It always has amused me that when I was required to study, I did not give it much effort. However, when I was driven by curiosity, there was no way to stop me.

One of the sweetest men in the world taught the class; always smiling as if he had a hanger in his mouth. Dr. Lloyd Cressman started the first semester with the Old Testament and the second semester was the New. We didn't really talk much doctrine, but philosophy was high on the agenda. It was one of the few subjects that impressed me as a college student.

I think of my journey as one from outer darkness to the light. It may seem strange when you read the story, but without a doubt you will know in your heart what it was, and require no drawn out explanation. For those who have had trouble accepting the existence of our Heavenly Father and His Son, wondering if my experience might provide enlightenment and strength, fear not: there could have been no one more skeptical or cynical than I, going into this.

About the story

This is a chronicle of difficult events and overwhelming anguish leading up to my baptism, the equally as extraordinarily hard year that followed, and subsequent trials that made me grateful for knowing the Lord was with me. Why? The incidents are examples of being "perfected" by bad times. Were I a sword I could be considered one of the hardest metal instruments on earth for all my tempering. There were challenges that made me question many things, but never my faith in the gospel, Christ Jesus, or our Father in Heaven. One of the great lessons of my saga is realizing some of the challenges we face do not come from Heavenly Father or even Satan: they can come from ourselves and sometimes those who think they serve Him: because even they are mortal with the frailties of mankind (and yes: some of our local leaders can be oblivious to their own arrogance. I should note this was a common theme across the country). However, a major point to recognize is that I was able to strengthen my resolve and testimony because there were a few leaders and priesthood holders who were awe-inspiring, righteous and inspired men in this walk over the hot coals of life.

I suspect if you speak to any convert who has determined to grasp the rod with both hands, each will tell you it was often a white knuckle experience through the first year and maybe even beyond. I can say with unyielding certainty that Lucifer is not an imaginary caricature: he is real. He has minions, there are many, and they are not stupid. I have lived among them, and know I do not want to rub shoulders with them again.

I make no excuses for my conduct prior to coming to Christ and His church. The circumstances under which I grew up certainly contributed to my thought processes, but I accepted long ago that I alone bear responsible for my actions.

I write this saga to help inspire those with drooping spirits, sagging faith, and the feeling they are stuck in a place no one wants to be. Perhaps you have been a practicing disciple but something has gone from your testimony; maybe it is all new to you and is overwhelming. I find it a terrible tragedy that those who initially believe, allow themselves to be swept up in doubt and dragged down into apathy or, worse, angst and anger. I am aware not all saints are active, and even those who are, may stray from the path. I think it's a lot easier being righteous if those around you are as well. That is not to say how good a saint, or even how good a person, you are depends on where you live: the same challenges wait, if not the temptations. People with sagging testimonies sometimes leave the church because of personal affronts, or watching iniquities in what we perceive as the righteous, or local leaders dismissing unfavorable behavior in their personal friendships. Again, I say to you: **DON'T**. Our faith can be tested in many ways. It is up to you to seek the Lord's guidance. **Give up prayer and you give up.**

This is a story I write in the first person because it is real, happened to me, and I need not hide behind the pen. I have laughed, cried, raged, and ultimately learned. I made mistakes and now can laugh at them. It may be taking a little longer for me to laugh at the malevolence of others for a while; though. I will start by making the observation that with some certainty; my tempering for a few decades may be described as, perhaps, a living Hell. I pray regularly I never return. However, it is likely I would not have found the church had circumstances not brought me to my knees. There was a purpose to it all. Why did Heavenly Father care enough to bring me back from the noxious abyss, to set me on the path laden with the sweet smell of righteousness? I cannot figure out and have stopped trying.

As I write this some years after the fact, I have come to learn much about the Mormon culture. That is vital, if you are a convert. The church has problems: but it is the people that cause them. Not all are strict adherents to the gospel (surprise!). Some make up their own rules (yeah: it happens among members and local leaders too). Others do no thinking on their own but can quote every thought uttered by an apostle or prophet. They fail to realize leaders up and down the line are mere mortals. They have opinions: and are not always correct when they express them. If you sincerely pray about something, you will know if what they offer is true. The church as an institution has taken some great strides to admit and set the record straight on misinformation of the past, and to address its recognition of problems inherent in a leadership of 30,000 wards/branches. It is not good form, in the leadership's minds, to aggressively repudiate erroneous statements of past apostles and prophets. So, understand this and be charitable. They are moving. It is a big institution and it takes time.

If a local leader is the cause of you questioning your testimony, think of it as a challenge. If it is untenable, find another ward. Don't put people above the worship of the Lord.

For the sake of privacy and to avoid embarrassment of some participants in this circus, most names have been changed.

In The Beginning

The journey was a long one, but I have come to understand each step was necessary for me to fulfill my destiny. The bitterness I experienced along the way served to give me an appreciation for the savor of life when it mattered most.

For many years I was a devout workaholic. My last full time job before my crash and burn often found me entering the building at 6 A.M. and not leaving until 7 P.M, plus a long commute to and from the heart of Brooklyn, New York to my home on the New Jersey shore. Seven days a week I devoted to work, in addition to occasional week nights. Additionally, every weekend found me also managing the affairs of an elderly friend. In the end, I was rewarded for neither loyalty nor sacrifice to my job or friendship. My social life was a void due to the demands of both work and friendship. I gave up my career only to have been deceived and left stripped of literally everything I owned, including my own self-worth. When it came time to re-enter the job market no one would hire me because I was out of work too long, being the loyal buddy. Cynicism is an inborn trait to many New Yorkers, and I was (perhaps still am) no exception. My personal motto had become no good deed goes unpunished.

After leaving active duty and then a few years out of Physician Assistant training, I took a temporary job at a nursing home. This was after realizing my then current employer was not running a sleep clinic; but a mill for Quaaludes. Those were drugs used to induce sleep, allegedly in the insomniac. But, they were more commonly pushed as high cost street drugs. I had a new car with payments and couldn't afford to take time off and be casual in looking for another position. I vowed to take the first job to come along. I went to the interview dressed in blue jeans, moccasins, and a denim vest. I obviously was foiled in my attempt to sabotage the interview because they hired me. It didn't appear to be hard work and I have always been amused by the elderly; so I decided to give it two years.

I became friendly with the medical director who was approaching her sixties. She was an interesting woman in her own right: though had some realllllyyyyy difficult personality traits, was married to a surgeon and they had no children. She had gone to nursing school after graduating high school early, and then decided to become a physician. Working her way through Columbia University School of General Studies for her undergraduate degree, as well as through medical school was rather unusual. Eunice really was an incredible woman for all she accomplished, although, like the rest of us mortals, had more than her share of character flaws.

I worked at the nursing home two years and moved on. She was irate, taking the action as a personal affront. She had a problem with reality and the status of physicians. The fact was that we had to work harder because the physicians she paired us with were incompetent, lazy, and only worked 20 hours of the 40 they were paid for. Not so funny was her belief that physicians were above criticism. When an M.D. appeared on TV after being arrested for murdering his wife, Eunice was incredulous that they took him away in handcuffs. You get the point, I am sure. She hailed from the generation called the golden age of medicine, where doctors could do no wrong. The advent of medical malpractice litigation pandemic took care of that fantasy.

Her ire with me probably would have lasted a lot longer if Pasqual, her husband, did not suffer a stroke. I took over managing their finances. She was brilliant academically but initially had no handle on financial matters, lacked "street smarts", appeared to live in an alternate reality, and additionally had no common sense.

Pasqual played the horses, high-stakes card games, and frequented Atlantic City enough to be known at the major casino hotels. There was not any considerable savings. In fact, Pasqual gambled away the retirement fund of the office practice. Eunie did not get angry at Pasqual; but she did resent the physician who left, when he demanded his share of the retirement. It actually went to litigation before Pasqual grudgingly paid him off. Soon after, Pasqual had a stroke. It probably saved my friend from financial ruin.

What there was left of their money, he had forgotten. I went through the horrendous bookkeeping and we invested, initially with the help of their financial advisor. I had her set up a 401k at work plus we implemented a few other investment strategies. Her husband lingered for 13 more years, progressively becoming vegetative. As brilliant as she was, the physician refused to accept her spouse required more than she could give him. I spent part of my weekends at her home, did her shopping, put up with her short temper, prejudices and idiosyncrasies. It also meant giving up any social life, and towards the end of Pasqual's mortality, leaving work to handle emergencies, or accompanying her places. Eunice did have a full time housekeeper and caregiver for Pasqual during week days, with part-time help on the weekends. She had little pity on them when they requested time off, and trusted no one.

In 1998 I was working for a physician practice management company, rising from manager to vice president of operations in a few years. It was a heady job but not without its own problems. Managing a large budget, more than 100 personnel and 13 clinics took time and energy. The politics were treacherous and I never liked or wanted to learn to play games. I was one of two women in the organization with some semblance of authority: and the other one was living with the majority stockholder. My boss thought he was paying me the highest compliment when he told someone he liked me because I thought like a man. It is safe to say the boys on 41st street thought it required testosterone to have intellect. That is probably why they were stunned when budget time rolled around and I requested a copy of the previous year's expenditures. I was told to just come up with what I could and someone would take care of it for me. I knew better than that, as appealing as it may have been.

The red flags went off a few months before, when an envelope filled with cash was inadvertently delivered to me because the intended party, their young golden boy attorney, was not in. The sealed envelope came from our headquarters in Manhattan, addressed to an all-too-familiar attorney running for political office. My assistant was asked to transport the parcel after I sent him uptown with some reports. They imagined Mark as being intellectually challenged, and had no problems talking in front of him about confidential matters. What they did not count on was his loyalty to me (and he was not as stupid as they imagined). My messenger watched while they stuffed the envelope with $10,000. He was eager to tell me exactly what was inside.

Those were the days of large dot-matrix printers spewing accordion-folded paper. My six foot tall runner delivered a stack almost up to his chin, after my nagging for more than a month. I was stunned when I looked at the bottom line, indicating my division was operating at a deficit. It took me a week to realize the reason we were in the red, in spite of having the largest receipts. We were being charged with all the payroll expenses for all the divisions, a private car service for a stockholder's nurse to travel from Virginia to New York, my bosses medications, eyeglasses, and salaries for the no show ex-wife, daughter, and daughter-in-law of the founder. His daughter-in-law received a nice paycheck just for being married to his son (I have to admit, that alone was worthy of pay). There was more to their cooking of the books. It was a certainty their manipulation of the stock would catch up with them despite the CEO dining regularly with the now scandalized head of the SEC. It did: but too bad no one was prosecuted as far as I know.

The company's first and largest business, my division, was an injury-related medical practice that diagnosed and treated patients in litigation. We provided expert witnesses for court testimony, usually for the plaintiff but sometimes the defense. Most patients were referred by specific attorneys, who were not concerned about justice; just playing the game and getting their cut. Once I became responsible for daily operations, and monitored payments, it became evident to me two things were not in keeping with good business practices (or ethics or the law). Most patients were advised by their lawyers not to provide any information regarding health or sometimes auto insurance (New York is a no-fault state). Those patients signed a contract to pay us in full once their case was closed: win or lose. When they lost, our financial men made sure the charges were written off. When plaintiffs won, they paid the bill: anywhere from one to ten cents on the dollar. That meant we ate the cost of all the MRIs the lawyers insisted upon, the salaries of the staff, physicians, physical therapists, etc.

Clients were usually those who had no significant case to start with. Our only regular payments were from worker's compensation claims, but the doctors were ordering unnecessary tests and treatments to run up the bills for the lawyers. Insurance carriers are an equally greedy lot so they would not pay for the excesses. Once a settlement was reached, the injured party miraculously was healed and we never saw them again. The lawyers generally got a small settlement, took their cut, and the deal was that we get no more cases if we go after the debt. The routine was to carry them as open files, even after the clients settled their pittance. If you are into investing, you will understand this was just to demonstrate there were considerable outstanding receivables to be recovered. It ran up the price of the stock, as they went for a second offering.

But let's get back to the story. Pasqual died in March of 98 and Eunice was recovering from hip surgery. Though there was a will, that document could not be found. We later learned from his brother that everything went not only to Eunice: also his first spouse. My friend walked away with everything.

She asked if I would help her find another place to live: in New Mexico. By that time PMC was taking a nose dive onto its own sword and would soon be delisted from the stock exchange. Sure enough, when we went out to look at real estate, the company went belly. I was out of work. We found a place for her and she was infatuated with the country as well as the real estate brokers, who we will call Trash and Crash.

She asked if I would move out there with her. I knew she'd never make it on her own and it would mean giving up a career. I said yes anyway, moving into a small studio on her property and later to my own house.

I could not find work. Everywhere I interviewed said they were afraid I'd leave as soon as a better paying job came along (getting a New York salary is not always an advantage). Eunie said not to worry; we were "partners" and she would leave everything to me anyway. That was probably one of the worst decisions ever made. I became that frog dropped into the pot before the heat was turned up. It was both amusing and annoying that all the legal papers in New Mexico described her as a "single woman". She found this offensive, wanting to be referred to as widow. When I explained she had no choice, she looked me straight in the eyes and said it

31

was an insult: as if marriage was an elevated status and I had not risen to her level so would not understand. I might add, that is also how I am viewed by some of our charitable LDS sisters, so it is universal I guess. On the few occasions I went out with men, she was worse than a jealous teenager.

I did contract work for a commercial photography company and some writing: but not enough to keep from going into my savings over the years. I spent most of my time taking care of her financial business, doing light handiwork repairs, projects in her house and something of a companion as well as caretaker. The financial advisor was of no use to us once we moved (nor actually while we were in New York), so I learned what I could. It became a nerve-wracking responsibility to care for what had become a large investment folder. When the market started to turn in the early part of the decade, I knew something was coming but did not know what to do. Fortunately I moved fast enough to put all her investments in nearly risk-free funds and took the brunt of scorn; until all her friends lost at least half the value of their portfolios. She was grateful temporarily, but annoyed the investments no longer yielded well over 10 percent.

My responsibilities included two poorly constructed, over-priced Koi ponds with waterfalls (you can tell she didn't always heed my counsel). You may think that New Mexico does not get cold, but it does. One year Eunie noticed ice had frozen solid in the big pond and feared the Koi would not have oxygen since the wooden block used to keep the water moving, was froze in place. We bought two trough heaters (used to keep water troughs from freezing) and hooked one up. The second was to be a backup, but my buddy determined that one was not enough. Of course it required someone (me) to break a hole in the ice before using the thing. For this purpose we bought hip waders.

Let no one tell you the cold cannot be felt through those things. I was wearing heavy wool socks and sweat pants. It was frigid enough that my legs had no sensation and I could not feel my nose or lips. As for keeping dry, they worked fine until I slipped on the ice on the bottom of the cement floored pond. I went under completely, wearing my new down vest, and could not get up. The water quickly soaked the vest, filled the boots, and drenched my sweatpants. Sensation returned to my lower extremities: pain. I had to crawl out on my abdomen because my legs were so heavy I could not lift them. My bare hands grasped for the ice covered boulders surrounding the slick cement steps, to no avail. I am sure I resembled a beached whale. Needless to say I was frozen. I got the boots off but then needed to get to my truck where I kept a gym bag with extra clothes (of course, not winter wear). Eunie offered no assistance. The wind was without mercy and it felt like I had icicles hanging from head to toe. After walking to the front door of the house, I was required to remove my clothes before entering because she did not want the tiled floor messed up. I went home dressed in my t-shirt, gym shorts, and old running shoes. It was 28 degrees out.

When we were there a few years, she said she'd like to be friends with Trash and her husband Crash. I invited them to lunch celebrating Eunie's birthday. Their relationship progressed and while I was noticing how much the couple resembled charlatans, she was being pulled under their control deeper and deeper. When I warned her about them, she told them and made insulting comments to me.

It culminated when she became gravely ill with temporal arteritis, and was put on high doses of steroids. The couple had been trying to create a dependence on them. I again tried to explain they were interested in more than just her dynamic personality. She asked me why I cared. I found that an incredulous question after 23 years of friendship; but responded that I had an emotional investment in her well-being. This brilliant woman took that to mean I was interested in her money; no doubt reinforced by her friends the grifters.

Long periods of high dose steroids often bring changes in mental status. Her personality had changed and they started playing hard ball, so to speak. I stood between them and Eunice's money; which they had lots of plans for. The pair was heavily invested in property they could not get rid of, living over their means, and he was a control freak. They wanted Eunice to buy property, which I regularly talked her out of for a while. When Eunie wanted to buy two parcels around her house, Trash brokered the deal. There were no negotiations and Trash took her full commission. Actually, Trash never negotiated: always telling Eunie that the sellers in New Mexico do not cut their prices. Of course, when Eunie sold a small investment house, Trash advised her to cut the price by about $5k, if I recall correctly.

Crash had been one of those TM or other mind twisting guru types in California when he met Trash. He also held himself to be a psychologist. The man gave Eunie a CD and had her listen to it every day. I have no doubt there were subliminal messages. On more than a few occasions she became emotional after listening.

Eunie, for all her faults, was usually a woman of integrity and honor (that business of her husband's will was startling to me). The more time spent with Trash and Crash, the more of a change I noticed. The worst of it all was that she began to lie. It was like she and her new friends were teenagers in their own exclusive sorority. Trash would intervene and just like a child, take sides when Eunie and I disagreed about something: important or otherwise. It was a symbiotic relationship for them. It went on ad nauseum. However, I threw her an 80th birthday celebration attended by her sister from California, and another couple, besides Trash and Crash: Betty and Frank. Betty wanted to be part of their little group although she had mixed feelings about Trash. I was warned by her several times that Trash's intention was to put me out of the picture.

Her sister and I watched the interaction with incredulity. We had been discussing Eunie's decline over the years and Ronnie made the observations herself, noting the growing control the charlatans were exerting. There were no real surprises for me at the dinner, but it was an eye opener for everyone else. It was the culmination of everything Satan's henchmen had hoped for. My erstwhile friend Eunice got up in the private dining room and told Trash and Crash how much they meant to her, how she never met anyone as wonderful as they, and no one had ever offered the friendship and caring that they did (I only gave up 23 years, a career, and autonomy).She would do anything for them, she said. She then went around the table briefly and pretty much said as an after-thought that the rest of us were okay. Betty and her husband sat in silent shock, while Ronnie was mortified. I was not at all surprised. The handwriting was on the wall. Crash was Eunie's Svengali. I was thinking that the light at the end of the tunnel was a train headed for me: with no way to escape it.

Not long after that, Trash got bold and consorted with Eunie over something stupid. They distressed me beyond where I could ignore. I had become a target and knew it. I was on the phone with Ronnie when I felt this crushing chest pain, but figured it was all a matter of mind over body. A month later I couldn't walk to the end of my driveway. I went to the cardiologist and it was diagnosed as a heart attack. I had quadruple bypass surgery a few months later. Trash and Crash stepped up the action and by June the triumvirate of Betty, Trash and Eunie stopped talking to me. When I needed people most, no one was there. After 23 years I became sick and expendable. The one thing that did surprise me was Betty. Trash and Eunie had somehow corrupted the one person I thought I could trust, but who was obviously following the gold too.

Suddenly, I was face to face with the speeding locomotive.

Eunie demanded I get out of her life. She technically owned the house I was living in and Trash told her she would get a good price for it. My former friend told me to take my time; and then two days later instructed me to be out in three weeks. I was advised she would give me a sum of money payable over 4 years. It was a paltry sum compared to what I would have had, but I accepted the offer. What choice did I have? It was quite clear she intended on leaving everything to Trash. In good times the portfolio and property were worth more than $2M. I took what I had and moved to Texas, where within 2 months Maxx, my sweet companion and cat, died suddenly of undetected cancer.

The saga doesn't end there. Ronnie had words with Eunie around 6 weeks after my surgery, about how the group of them had all hung me out to dry. I knew by then Trash and Crash had broken any bonds between Eunie and her sister, as well as me. The sisters spoke to each other weekly until Eunie died, about 2 years later. Ronnie did not learn until the end that Eunice was leaving everything to Trash and not so much as a keepsake for Ronnie. In fact, there was a specific paragraph saying she was to get nothing. Ronnie is still reeling.

In the meanwhile, my health deteriorated after the heart attack and by-pass surgery. A few weeks after surgery, the stress had its impact and I was back in the hospital: one of the grafts had failed. I was dead spiritually and knew it, realizing it was just a matter of time before my body followed. The hole I had been digging for myself over many years became deeper and my soul turned to a frozen mass in the absence of light. I had no doubts the life I had lived to that point was unworthy of forgiveness, and I was quite certain it was payback time for ignoring what I knew to be the teachings of Christ.

It took no courage for me to debate politics with passion; but when it came to the Heavens, I was conspicuously quiet. It was only justice in my mind that I paid for my willingness to keep the peace with Eunie and her friends rather than stand up for what I knew in my heart. How many times I sat still saying nothing when Crash would speak of a force controlling our lives but categorically state it was not God. My mouth remained shut when the deity and even existence of Christ was questioned. I pretended not to hear when different ethnic and racial groups were "proven" inferior by using the scriptures. I was silent on the outside; yet my mind was screaming for me to stand up and tell them to shut up. Yes, it was payback that was coming to me; I deserved it and just wanted to die.

I was not going to stay in New Mexico, given the circumstances. I had started a relationship with a man who lived in Texas. I was not stupid enough to move near him, but rented a place about 3 hours away, north of Dallas. That, of course, did not work out. He was a nice guy but not someone I wanted to spend the rest of my life with.

I had not yet unpacked everything when Maxx went to his final rest, and decided there was nothing except bad memories for me in Texas. My Physician Assistant certification had lapsed and I did not feel prepared to re-certify. A lot had transpired since leaving my career. I knew that if I had trouble finding work when I first got to New Mexico, it would be no easier years later in Texas. No matter where I applied or for what, no one wanted me. I sent out hundreds of job applications and got no response from any. My dedication and years spent caring for my friend were obviously not viewed as strength of character. The unsung song was that I was too old and not actually employed, for too long.

Where would I be likely to find a job and not be considered too old? Florida! I put everything in storage and moved on to the land of sunshine and retirees; where I wandered and interviewed for several months. Of course my timing was exceptional, if my intellect was not. It was right after Hurricane Katrina and all the refugees from the storm were looking for work too. Things went from bad to worse.

I was alone and in an abyss so deep I stopped looking for even a flicker of hope. I was breathing but I was not living. I was waiting for the first of the year to receive the money owed me. It was getting tight financially. My health insurance from New Mexico cut me off: I was not living in-state. I had exhausted all the free nights I accumulated from motel stays, and it was Christmas time. My brother, who had a house in New York as well as a town house in southern Florida, and I used to email frequently. He happened to be in Florida for the holidays. The day before Christmas I told him I would probably not be able to use my email for a few weeks because I had to leave where I was. What I was paying for the temporary residence was going to be needed for food. I was out of money and about to be living in my car until the check came through. I explained also, that my Christmas dinner was a can of tomato soup. His response the next day was a collection of pictures showing him and his family having dinner at his in-laws. The table was filled with all the fixings and their Christmas presents. He merely said "okay". My brother said nothing of my situation, offered no help, encouragement, and certainly not an invitation to stay at his place. That was okay: I probably would not have wanted me around either.

Prior to that demonstration of Christian charity, I sat motionless in my car with my loaded revolver in my lap. The gun was only a .32 caliber but sufficient, I thought, to do what needed to be done. It was quite appropriate to use my friend's weapon to end what had become a never ending nightmare she initiated. I hit emotional bottom as I sat in my car watching the rain sheet over the windows. I inhaled the cigarette held between trembling fingers of my right hand, watching the smoke spread across the roof and exiting the small openings of the front windows; while my left hand caressed the final solution. The things that passed through my mind were not rife with blame for others, or wishing someone would stop me. The concerns were things like who would clean my car of the blood and brains? Would that decrease the value of it since the

SUV was only six months old? Should I write a suicide note? Who should I write it to? Did anyone care? Then, there was the question of my competency. As a child I contemplated suicide on a number of occasions but had been convinced by my parents that I was too inept to do anything right. The same fear of failure came back to haunt me. I was afraid I'd become one of those statistics where the patient doesn't die right away, becoming a vegetable for decades. I thought I would be more successful starving to death, which was a real possibility.

Come the first of the year when I expected a check from Eunie, there was nothing. I wrote, and Trash responded in her capacity as an attorney. She began by telling me I was extorting money from a helpless old lady. In addition she said half a million dollars was unaccounted for. Considering I intentionally never had direct access to the money or power of attorney, if money was missing it was whoever took over her affairs after I was gone; though I doubt any money was gone at all. To make matters worse, because I was traveling I used my cousin's address in New Jersey for correspondence with Eunie. Trash sent my cousin my note and a letter to her as well, indicating she would be sued for complicity. I was enraged and responded to Eunie but never heard another word. We had an oral agreement because I wanted no more contention. She initially wanted a written contract and I agreed to it. I suspect Trash talked her out of that. What could I do? Not much. However, as I look back I can even see the Lord's sense of humor in this.

As I said previously, I never had access to her money. That she left everything to Trash was in no way a surprise to the charlatan. What happened when she finally got her hands on the fortune probably had her swearing mightily. I take you back a few years. I had my friend heavily invested in tax-deferred funds, including a hefty IRA. Trash must have been shocked to learn she would nowhere near that windfall, because of taxes.

I wondered what else was left for me. I found out shortly thereafter. My cousin decided I was a negative force in her life and cut off communications.

One more thing, since we are talking about another gut-wrenching visit to Satan's humble abode. With Ronnie's permission, I did Eunie's ordinances. Did she deserve it? Not my decision.

44

The Even Longer Road Traveled

The words of two television evangelists had struck a chord right after Maxx passed away, and their messages were now resounding in my mind. The emotional pain was unbearable. I thought about the preachers. Why not? It was then I prayed. I was not sure how to do it, but offered my soul. I needed help and had no where else to turn. I made it easy for Him too. I pleaded to take me, knowing it would mean a place other than Heaven. I didn't care. I was already in a living Hell and couldn't imagine it being any worse than living with Satan's progeny as I had been doing for seven years. I needed the pain to stop. The only constant in my life had been my Maxx and the little guy no longer needed me. He was the one being who helped me maintain what little sanity I knew I had left.

But, the Lord wasn't about to put my request in the express bin. I assumed I had more suffering to do before my prayers would be granted. In fact, I was destitute because the funds which I expected from Eunie never came. I couldn't find work but needed medication for my heart and diabetes. I reluctantly found refuge in my mother's home back in New York. She was retired and on a limited fixed income. She could provide food and shelter. The rest was up to me.

For 6 months I rolled up in the fetal position and kept the bedroom door closed, waiting to die; praying for it. I was too weak to do much more than walk down the hallway once in a while to eat dinner. Then I decided I had to get work.

I borrowed money to take a real estate license class and the exam. I passed with flying colors: on the week the housing market crashed. For some reason I was encouraged to join a new real estate agency in a different county, who promised new and innovative approaches as well as equally sharing leads with all the agents. I was the first person they took in: and the last to get any leads. The one lead I received will always be a classic in my mind. There was a potential buyer wanting to see a summer cottage in a remote community. I did not yet own a GPS and looked it up online. Following the instructions took me to the middle of a vacant field: where I could not get a cell phone signal.

After getting that squared away with the office, I met the man, who had seen the property two years before, when it had been damaged by wildlife. The new owners were asking $40k for the small cabin with no running water. It received water during the summer from the stream out back. It also could not have a well drilled since it would be too close to the neighbor's septic tank. The place was off of a regular road, on an unpaved one. The buyer did not want to put any money down, demanded a no document mortgage at a low rate of interest. Around here there are very few banks making loans for less than $60k, and even fewer for seasonal homes in undeveloped areas. I spent several days calling all of them. None wanted to do it on the buyer's terms.

About that time, the real estate agency decided to try a new marketing tactic. They brought onboard a very personable gay man. With him, they began sending buses down to New York City, organizing tours of new communities in the area. They had events targeted to gays, and excluded the rest of us from any transactions with them. We could attend the events, staff the informational booth, but that was it.

I left for another agency, as a last shot. Again, I was promised the world. I had to attend weekly personal tutoring sessions with the owner in his Pennsylvania office. I had a bad feeling about my move, and knew why when he merely wanted me to go find the clients; and he would do the deal. I would get a finder's fee of sorts, and not the commission.

On my way back that night I became violently ill, winding up in a local hospital. The place was a zoo and I was sure I was going to get my wish to die, fulfilled.

I had enough of real estate; but what was I qualified for? It was costing me money to do real estate, having to pay for gas, ads, seminars, open houses, etc.; besides, walking and climbing stairs had become a nightmare.

One day I was reading and wondering what high school student wrote the piece: it was terrible. A thought occurred to me that I could do far better.

Whether the effort was stellar or not, it was far superior to much of the stuff I was reading. Suddenly, I was capable of doing work I would never have imagined. My former English teachers and professors would have bet their life savings I could not become a professional writer. So would I. It made me think very hard. It did not escape my attention that this new found ability had to be a God given talent: but why would He bless me?

The life of a non-fiction writer is not glamorous, nor is it lucrative. Fiction is even worse unless you happen to be well-known and have a good imagination. I am in

48

possession of neither characteristic. I am so uncreative people often have to explain jokes to me. That left me to write about things I knew or could learn. It is very hard for new writers to crack the markets and I was no exception. Some of the jobs I took are an embarrassment now; but at that time they permitted me the opportunity to at least afford insulin over-the-counter. I had been hoarding insulin pump supplies so I was good for a while in that department. It was not until I wound up in the hospital cardiac step-down unit that I obtained some of the cardiac meds I had done without; although it was only a week's supply. Still it made a difference for a short period and I was signed up for Medicaid, much to my chagrin. If I had any pride left at that point, the nightmare of applying for medical assistance destroyed it. It had been almost an entire year without heart medications and I miraculously survived. First year cardiac patients who do not take their medications have a 20% chance of surviving to their first anniversary. Add lack of adequate insulin to tweak those odds. I should have been dead. I was intent on a lethal exodus, but didn't want to suffer; and believe me when I tell you being short of breath walking more than ten feet, struggling up a flight of steps, and being unable to breath at night, is not pleasant. Rather than see it as a miracle, I thought this was the ultimate rejection of the Lord. Even HE didn't want me.

My life has been quite an example of Murphy's Law. I was plagued by intractable pain down my leg since the Texas move; and it reached the point where no amount of drugs or spinal blocks would relieve the incredible torture. It hurt to walk, stand, sit, and lie down. There was no position that was comfortable. It was determined I had spondolithesis: where the vertebrae slide over each other trapping the nerves of the spinal cord. Reluctantly it was to the operating room where they fused the vertebrae with hardware. Following a period of regret, I ultimately recovered and life without pain day and night, was a whole new experience and a lot brighter. I also began to notice and think about the reversal of some of my trials and the gift of being able to write, was not by virtue of anything I did. It was the first time I realized the Lord had shown me His love. Life was not great; but the train had passed and I was still around to tell the tale.

Welcome

I do not know exactly why the transformation occurred, but a few more months after surgery I abandoned my daily routine of curling into a ball, praying for death.

I was getting more writing gigs and after selling my camera, had enough to take a course in editing; then I attended a course for grant writers. By this time, I knew it was the hand of the Lord, and decided I had a gift that might improve the life of others. I started writing grants for small worthy non-profit groups; pro bono. I also taught some of them how to do it their selves.

Oddly, after so many years of being alone, I wanted company. I signed up for one of the larger dating services and after a number of out and out losers, met someone living in New Hampshire. We shared similar political values, were both avid conservatives and Romney fans (which at times may sound like an oxymoron). He invited me to visit and then to attend the Dartmouth homecoming festivities. We had pleasant weekends and continued the relationship. The man was someone to talk to, debate with, and do things I hadn't done in years; normal conversation being one of them. Up until then I had forgotten what freezing at a football game was, sitting in nosebleed seats at hockey games, and even enduring jazz bands (not particularly my thing, but he liked the stuff). We went with Mitt to hand in his New Hampshire primary papers in Manchester, cheered at his rallies, and I was in the world of the living; perhaps really enjoying life for the first time ever. It didn't matter to me that I no longer had all the toys and emblems of success.

One evening we were debating the merits of formal religion and the hierarchal structure. I saw formal religion as another political power game played by men. That being said, I didn't find any particular comfort in the idea of women priests or ministers either. I just did not believe anyone should or could tell me about God the Father or His Son Jesus Christ.

In retrospect, it is indeed interesting that I innately knew there is a Father who has a divine Son. I had always held that the Bible was a corrupt collection of parables and allegories passed on much like the game of telephone, where the initial message is changed dramatically from first to last. The oral tradition existed long before the written one for ancient texts, and who could trust it? In my thinking, Paul was a chauvinist, I knew how the Hebrews and early Christians decided what belonged in the tome and most of it was politically expedient for propagation of the faith or government rule. I questioned why there were so many versions of the old and new testaments if the collection was all the word of God. I did not understand why television evangelism should make millionaires of their ministers, and trusted neither the people nor institutions.

In between our glasses of red wine he passionately gave testimony of a church needing leadership and the man in charge being the intermediary for God. I was incredulous that such an intelligent man should come up with such a stupid idea. My response was that if he believed so strongly, why had he not been to church for years? It sounded rather hypocritical to me. The reply, after a brief pause to reflect, was that he would go, if I went with him. This was not an anticipated or welcome response. Every church or synagogue I ever entered made me terribly uncomfortable. I had fallen into the trap intended for him, and I had to agree.

Services were held on Sundays, which I thought a novel approach in contradiction to the ever popular Saturday evenings. Giving up my Sunday was going to be a sacrifice, especially since the weather was threatening and I had a 4 hour ride back to New York. I would have to get up early for the 10 o'clock service, in addition to hitting the road later for the drive on the Taconic Parkway in the dark. I also had to buy a long skirt, according to Ron: since it wasn't a casual dress sort of place. How weird! Dressing up for church? This commitment was getting complicated.

The following Sunday we got out of bed, went for the breakfast buffet where we each additionally downed a few cups of java to start the day, and headed for the church. Before we got there, Ron announced he was Mormon. Given his lifestyle of smoking, drinking coffee, beer, wine, and other activities we need not explore, even I knew it was inconsistent with traditional LDS decorum. I was a bit anxious about the day ahead, since what little I did know about Mormons was that they were very different. It never occurred to me, as it did to some, they were a cult, but they had odd ideas. What I remembered the most about them were the Nixon aides. However I felt about formal religion, I envied anyone who could believe like that; and thought it would be worth the effort if it helped bring an estranged man back to his faith.

The first thing I noticed about the building, inside and out, was the simple design with practicality. There were no crosses, ornate glass, silver or gold inlay, etc. It was so different without the usual distractions of a traditional church building. Walking into the hallway on that very cold morning, we were greeted by a short, elderly gentleman with a mane of bold white, who apparently recognized Ron. Though people greeted him as bishop, I later learned he was actually the patriarch. After inquiring about Ron's father, the man grasped my hand in greeting with both of his. His warmth was startling. To this day I do not have a clue what he said. I was enveloped or maybe it was even embraced, by an intangible presence and love. It was oddly familiar but now think I must not have known it since before the womb; because it was certainly unknown in this mortality. I thought I heard whispering "welcome home". Stunned is one way to describe it, although at the time I was sure it was a psychotic break. I said nothing, not knowing what I could say or who to tell. As unfamiliar and scary the event was, I did not want the experience to end.

As we entered the chapel, Ron told me to follow his lead, emphasizing that I be sure to take the sacrament with my right hand and pass it that way too. I am amazed at remembering those two things so distinctly and not knowing what else transpired in the meeting. I find it strange now that he considered etiquette so important. What I didn't grasp then, but realized later, was that happened to have been fast and testimony day. As I relay this story to you, I am still mortified. I shudder to think of what I did, not knowing the meaning of either the sacrament or fast.

More was in store for me though. You might be interested to learn I grew up within walking distance of the local meeting house, the only one in the county. The county itself was small, in spite of being heavily populated by IBM. We could always count on two young men from the church at our door at least yearly. Notwithstanding my parents both being "cultural Jews", I was always interested in learning about Christianity, and comparative religion fascinated me. I received the Book of Mormon several times in my life, and thought it a nice collection of someone's imagination, just like other scriptures; no worse than any other theological writ. The thought that the Lord had been giving me hints and opportunities over the years, does not completely escape me. Looking back, it is like those commercials for a popular vegetable drink, where someone slaps their head to get their attention.

As we sat down in Sunday school that day, I listened to the discussion. My heart began to race and I was having a hot flash. Given I was well past my years of menopause, it should not have occurred. The anxiety set upon me when I realized my mind was accepting the book and doctrine as fact. Back at William Penn College where I developed the interest, I gained a testimony of Christ; but also became quite cynical in the interpretations of the different denominations. Unlike my soliloquies of the past on all the scriptures, now I KNEW the books were based in fact although with great literary license, allegories, and parables. More than that, the Book of Mormon was not a work of fiction. Joseph Smith was more than a kid who said he found some plates in the ground.

For the next few months I attended Sunday school with a new approach to the scriptures. I also quickly accepted that the lifestyle I was engaged in with Ron was contrary to the teachings of the Savior, and felt guilty partaking of the sacrament. My enigma was partially reduced when I convinced myself I was not a member and took no oath. Ron, evidently, found no such contradiction.

We became friendly with a couple who had migrated from the New York metro area years prior. Harold had borne a number of leadership mantles through his years, and was, maybe not by chance, born Jewish. He and his spouse became my teachers. In effect, they became my remote Home Teacher and Visiting Teacher. The man was a brilliant and learned scripture master, and also assessed the situation with Ron rather quickly.

To me, there was not much of a choice. I told Ron I was going to join the church as soon as I got my act together. Smoking, tea, and coffee were a mainstay of my life. My companion instructed me to wait: "let them come to you". That was not the correct answer and pretty much sealed our fate. After New Year's Eve in Vermont, I gave up the three loves of my life and one pleasantry: coffee, tea, smoking, and Ron, in that order.

He was the vehicle the Lord used to bring me to the church, and remained a friend for a while: but more about that later. The man knew the teachings better than I. I wish I could tell you he is on his way to repentance, but unfortunately not. Ron finds the life "too demanding" although acknowledging it is the true church. He has been attending more often than before we met, and participates in some of the ward functions, occasionally even bringing a new girlfriend. The ward brethren have provided physical help when he was remodeling his home, and now he has a Home Teacher. That's progress, I guess, since he's not totally a lost sheep. Ron still smokes, drinks coffee, beer, and wine. He does not abide by tithing, and finds the temple too ritualistic. I guess he's a cafeteria Mormon.

I did not go to church for a few weeks after leaving Ron, trying to gather nerve to walk into the local building. I knew I would be one of very few single women. It never mattered to me in the past. Yet it had become an issue that made me uncomfortable. In the real world it makes little difference these days; it is not such a minor thing in a relatively closed society nestled in the mission field. I thought many times about what life would be like for me in a family-centric environment and cringed. However, going to church was not optional. I had to step out of my comfort zone. One Sunday I planned to go, but rolled over in bed when the alarm went off. I wasn't ready. That afternoon I suffered from a guilty conscience that was not relenting for an entire week. The following Sunday I forced myself up the longest seven steps I ever trod, to enter the meeting house. There, on a sofa facing the plate glass doors, were two young men in dark suits with name tags, and a slightly older man leaning against the wall. One of the youngsters stood up and asked if he could help. I inquired who I was to see about being baptized. His mouth was gaping as his companion looked up in disbelief, wanting to know what I said. Then the older man turned to see what was happening. He too stared blankly as they started to mumble amongst themselves, like a scene from an Abbot and Costello routine. It was amusing since none of the three seemed to know what to do from there. As I got closer to the younger pair, I realized they were missionaries. I had heard of elders but never came in contact with any before, other than the boys in suits who knocked on the doors when I was young.

I was shown to the chapel and chose to sit in the back. Soon after, the two elders sat down near me. I imagined they were afraid to let me out of their sight. At the end of the sacrament meeting, I was leaving the chapel when the bishop approached and asked if I was visiting. I said "no: I'm here to stay." The man, who I have come to know as never being speechless, also stood with his jaw dropped and nothing came out for a while. After getting over the initial shock, the bishop and others realized it was real. I provided the name of the couple who had been sort of my remote Home Teachers, and he spoke to the Vermont bishop as well. I was baptized the following week.

As for Ron, we had some contentious moments in the intervening years, and it was best to end it after a few incidents. It is not without its amusement either. He did not understand why he does not have a calling; especially in the Primary. I suggested his lack of regular attendance, disdain for the Word of Wisdom, and being a poor example would be my guess. The smoking and drinking were just a bonus.

He wrote one day (do not think he ever used the phone) saying he would be down my way to pick up an old radial arm saw he bought on eBay, not far from here,. For what it would cost to drive his truck down I am sure it was not the wisest move. Never the less, I agreed to show him how to get there. He does not use a GPS, know what a Google map is, or own a cell phone. He also does not plan well; since no one was at the place we were to pick it up.

We went to a favorite diner of mine, where we had lunch and he talked endlessly about himself. He criticized the church concluding with a statement that the brethren had no right to ask us to be chaste. That was one of the highlights. My patience had been tested beyond endurance and I heard enough. We used my phone to finally contact the sellers. I later wrote him a note responding to all the comments that irked me, as well as expressing my humiliation when I learned the meaning of sacrament and how he knew chastity was required. I criticized him and he wrote back telling me he takes criticism from no one. He writes them off his list, said the man. There is a reason he has been divorced three times.

Apparently he did not have enough. After about a year I started to get emails from him explaining economics in regard to the latest comments by political hacks. It was gratifying to know it was not just me, but 4 other were included. I ignored the first diatribe. The next time, I asked why he found it necessary to deliver a lecture to a well-educated audience as if we were high school sophomores. I pointed out the political rhetoric was just that: and he needed to get a hobby. I think we are finally finished: he told me to go to Hell. He completed his rant by asking me what gives me the right to voice my opinion. That was a perfect opening: I simple said "I get paid for it". Oh, one more thing. I hit the "reply to all" icon and quite unexpectedly received praise from several of the other recipients.

I came to the church in a different way, and learned the precepts as they describe: line upon line. That doesn't always come on a timetable. I look back and laugh at that first week. Church met in the morning, and prior to joining, in the afternoon my dog and I had a routine. We would stop at Dunkin Donuts where I would get a large coffee and bran muffin, drive up to a national park, take a walk, and return. The week following my baptism I was proud of myself because I had switched to drinking decaf with my muffin. When we got home I was humiliated to realize my two big errors: the first being coffee, caffeine or not. The bigger mistake was in not understanding we do not buy anything on the Sabbath. I was in the church a week and had already screwed up!

My Formal Education

I started with the gospel fundamentals class for a few months. I had already read the scriptures, including the Book of Mormon, and became bored with the discussions in class. They were so elementary and devoid of intellectual discourse. In Vermont the regular Sunday school was informative, enlightening, and comfortable. I only mention this because it was my first challenge within the church. I decided to go back to what I thought I could benefit from, which was the regular Sunday school. At that time, while not exactly a free-wheeling forum, knowledgeable members voiced their thoughts and opinions, which I enjoyed.

However, the fundamentals teacher said I needed to stay in her class for a year. There was no doubt in my mind this had become personal to her. I found her leadership and skills lacking. Actually, her ineptness flowed from making the class about her personal life and I was not interested in it. I apologized, saying I didn't think the other students had read the Book of Mormon and grasped its principles or understood the gospel; while the ones in Sunday school had. It was not a matter of me being any more intelligent than those in her class. It was a matter of just sitting there versus being involved. I am not a teenager and I wasn't in high school.

Right after General Conference I discovered the BYU broadcasting site. To me it was tantamount to finding hidden treasure. I had the opportunity to listen to discussions that expanded my comprehension of the LDS take on all the sacred works. These were people who offered alternative views to that which I had known or heard. Ancient scripture took on a life of its own and reading Isaiah after hearing it dissected by these brothers and sisters gave it meaning I never imagined. Add to that the Sperry Symposium, Educational Week talks, the frequent retelling of the life of our recent prophets, and I could carry on an informed conversation. Best of all was my meandering brought me to the works of Hugh Nibley!

As for the sister teaching that class, not quite a year later she had a disagreement with the bishopric when her 26 year old son was deemed not ready to go on a mission; and the family went inactive. It taught me that the natural man and pride can still rear its ugly head even in the church. Yes, before you say it, I was naïve.

Reality

I often recall the statement by President Hinckley indicating he never heard a talk he did not learn from. He never attended sacrament in our ward. However, once in a while even the most boring speaker can come up with a topic worthy of thinking about. One Mother's day happened to bring us food for thought. It was not the typical salute to motherhood, and it was not particularly well-delivered: but it did not have to be. I just wonder how many got the message.

A childless sister recounted a few experiences with members making comments regarding that condition. Male and female can be thoughtless and rude when they want to know when the couple would fulfill their obligatory role as parents. The incident was not isolated. I have known parents of two children being castigated by members for not having more. There is also a certain pomposity among a good number of married couples and their interactions, or lack of them, with single and divorced women in the church. To be sure, not all are world-class yentas. I am not aware by what Christian principle they feel enabled and even obligated to be so passively aggressive and believe they are righteous. At Stake Conference not too long ago, a sister gave a talk on marriage. In it she described how sisters who do not wed will be denied exaltation. Not one of the leaders corrected the statement. In fact, no one even noticed.

Yes: people pay attention to what is important to them. Unfortunately, sometimes they worry about offending people politically: but rarely spiritually.

Finding a Partner

I was prepared to spend the rest of my life in solitude, especially since my requirements for an appropriate mate had skyrocketed from compatible and stable to all that and Mormon. I needed a worthy priesthood holder and learned quickly what a rare commodity that is in the latter stages of life. A few pings and dents were okay, given I am far from perfect. The problem was that as sisters get older, many brothers of the same age look for younger women to restore their lost youth, and to bring more children into the world. They also seem to drop off the roles faster than the sister saints. To tell the truth, there is not a wealth of worthy and available seniors out there. The LDS dating sites are heavily laden with divorced men that one soon learns have been to the altar multiple times: and for good reason. Yes, there are widowers; but this tends to pose two problems for me, though perhaps not for others. You are always compared to their sainted eternal partners, who are remembered for all their endearing qualities; and rightly so I guess. The more important issue to me is that I do not have a testimony of plural marriage in this life or the next. Being sealed to more than one partner is not wrong; it is just not something I want to do.

Frequently in General Conference we receive a message about the sisters in the church and how the apostles and First Presidency loves us all. For the righteous who have not had the opportunity to wed, they say, we are promised exaltation and families in the Celestial Kingdom. I believe it because the Prophets have said so: but it is still a hard concept to wrap my mind around from a practical standpoint. On the other hand, I am confident I will have an eternal companion there. The problem is the challenge in this mortality.

Over the past few years I have been contacted by worthy and not-so-worthy brethren seeking companionship. When I joined the church I had this not so brilliant idea of signing up for several LDS singles websites. What an experience! Having never been sealed, I am a commodity to some, and one that is in short supply. Within days I had proposals. Did any of them know me? Talk to me? See me? Do they know I have a legendary sharp tongue, low tolerance for nonsense, and absolutely no patience for those who wield their priesthood like a flaming sword?

It did not matter: they wanted someone NOW. I can recall one brother to whom I patiently explained that yes, it may be selfish.

However, I want a monogamous relationship and do not want to be spouse number 2 or 42: Brigham, Joseph, and others notwithstanding. This brother said he was my last chance at entering the Celestial Kingdom, and I was doomed for rejecting a worthy offer. This pronouncement came from an honorable priesthood holder living in the heart of Happy Valley.

I know widowers who love their eternal companions still, and cannot fathom the idea of remarrying. If some other sister or brother has a testimony of multiple marriages on either side of the veil, more power to them: I do not.

There are positives and negatives of online dating in general and even more so for saints. Among the problems are not the brothers and sisters who have been divorced once or twice, but the ones who keep making the same mistakes. Marry one of them and you are destined to become a notch on their belts. Just as a personal example, Ron had been divorced three times. He was good, for a while, as a friend: but eternity would have been too long.

Loneliness is tolerable, but man was not created to be content in that situation. We are not felines or any other genetic family who thrive on isolation and solitude. Marriage was not high on my list of priorities until joining the church. I was so busy it didn't matter. There wasn't room in my life for a man who would also make demands of my time.

As a Saint, I lived far from Happy Valley, out in the hinterlands of New York State. There weren't even enough single brothers in the stake to make a singles event viable. If you saw who showed up at the combined stake events for over 30 singles, you might well come away with the notion that you wasted your time. The chances of finding an eternal partner locally were slim to none.

Reptilia

After several months of trying a few Mormon sites, I went to one of the major non-sectarian dating dot coms. That is where I met Brother Wonderful from Saratoga Springs, Utah. He was very anxious to get married and appeared to have the right credentials: high priest, temple recommend. His history was a bit uncomfortable though. He said he was divorced twice: once from a non-member and the second an ex-communicated sister missionary. I never did grasp the details because of his communication inadequacy at times (later learning it happened when he lied: all the time). What I did understand was that his previous spouse was mentally ill and stripped him of all his assets. It sounded rather typical for a bad divorce. He said she was unstable and three psychiatrists advised him to get out of the marriage at any cost. The woman was described as pure evil.

What a whirlwind. William asked me to marry him and I accepted. I prayed about it but had yet to learn to differentiate between my imagination and that small voice. I was in a quandary and had reservations but decided it would be an adventure. That was the only thing I got right.

All was going well as we spoke of the future and rebuilding his seminar business. He portrayed himself as a world-wide management expert, based on a successful sales career in the pharmaceutical industry. He retired after bilateral hip replacements, and said he could no longer travel as much as was required. It was then he appeared to have joined the church and later met his second wife. They launched a career operating a company who provided experts to businesses for two day business seminars. I never did figure out why he gave that up. Of course it wasn't until later that reality reared its head: he was an employee; not an owner.

William had a notion that with the right partner he could write a New York Times best seller. From his emails it was clear he definitely needed help writing, despite claiming a Master's degree (which later was amended as "almost") from a well-known Philadelphia business school. His subject matter was business accounting and leadership. Since he had been out of the business for a number of years, had little in the way of academic credentials, and was teaching business math a few days a week at a local junior college, I knew he was unrealistic about writing a book (actually 3 little math books and a larger leadership tome); let alone a best seller. I didn't mind the dreams. He said he was financially secure despite the divorce, so we could afford to take the time on his project.

Will may have been a bit unrealistic, but he had all the outward signs of being committed to the faith. At the time, I was approaching my sixth month mark. Neither of us wanted to wait for a temple marriage. Had I waited, it would have obviated all the subsequent angst. In retrospect, I should have known that if he was faithful, we would not have been in a rush.

Even odder were other attitudes. I was looking forward to a patriarchal blessing. It struck me as more than strange that he never had, nor wanted, one. Still, there was so much I did not know about the church I dismissed it. Who wouldn't want one? Of course when he told me, after we were married, that the Lord told him he didn't need one and that he would be great (or something like that), I had my first misgivings about his sanity.

He spoke of flying to New York, marrying, and driving back to Utah in my SUV with a trailer behind us. First it was on a Tuesday: but that was moving too fast. Then it became Thursday: he suddenly had things to do. Friday he still had not purchased tickets for the following Monday night; as we watched the cost sky rocket from $359 to over $1000. Tickets were going to be hard to come by with BYU and the U of U fall semester soon starting. He was procrastinating and I was cynical. Finally on Sunday he said he was going to be flying out the following evening. During the previous week I had a hitch installed in anticipation of the trailer rental. He reassured me he would cover the cost of the move since I could not afford it. I did not reserve the trailer though. The hitch cost around $400, and being the trusting soul I am, I would not lay out the $600+ to rent one until he was standing in front of me.

Monday morning Will phoned to say he received a call from his doctor telling him he had terminal cancer and would die in three months; so marriage probably wasn't worth it. When I heard the diagnosis I knew something didn't make sense and didn't believe him or the prognosis. I was distrustful as a gut reaction. If it were true, why had he not told me there was a suspicion of it as we talked over the preceding weeks? It is not a diagnosis made on the first visit. However, as the sisters heard about it they asked if I was going out west to be with him. I began to feel guilty: I was reacting as a cynical New Yorker and not a Christ-like Molly Mormon. I didn't know what to do, but ultimately decided no one should die alone and determined I would go out there to join him if he consented. He agreed and said my mother would be paid back for what I had to borrow. It was then I realized I only had the address to his UPS store mail box, and not the house number. I thought it was odd, but learned Will was not very run-of-the-mill in anything.

Meanwhile, I was under contract to write three articles a week and my check due at the beginning of the month had not yet arrived: it was already two weeks late. I had to borrow the cost of traveling.

My instincts told me there was more to the story of his illness. Experience taught that most people freeze with fright when they get a cancer diagnosis. The man I thought I was in love with, did not project that attitude. It surprised me he did not even know what tests were done or what the results were. My immediate reaction was to find an oncologist at Huntsman, who specializes in prostate cancer. Having done so, I gave Will the number to call and arrange an appointment for after I arrived Thursday.

Driving alone with a dog was not something I was foreign to. However the circumstances of the venture were making me uneasy. I did not have the time or inclination to rent a trailer, so I loaded the SUV with the vitals, and also wedding gifts to be delivered to my bishop's daughter in Provo. We headed out and not a mile from my home made a short stop. Everything shifted, covering my four-legged companion, Drummer. I pulled over and repacked, neither of us the worse for wear. The dog merely looked at me and I imagined him thinking about how much more he will have to endure with this trip. I wondered if it were an omen of things to come. My theory was that if Will died or it did not work, I would be back. If it did work out, then we would all return to pick up the rest of my stuff.

William called almost hourly to track my progress. It was nice to know someone cared that much, although it was getting annoying as well. Somewhere after Ohio he stopped calling. I was relieved and the irritation ceased: until I reached Chicago sometime around midnight and found I no longer had my cell phone. That was the least of it. There was construction at the interchange. It provided a needed laugh when I recalled they were doing road work in the same place the last time I was in the Windy City: more than 20 years before. However, I was lost having forgotten to load the correct maps into the GPS (yes: the device was old). I found a pay phone to report my lost cell phone to the company, and need for a new one. I tried reaching William, but he had no listed number. That was strange. Why have an unlisted number unless you are a public personality, or in a profession that would warrant such privacy? There were other William Richards but not in Saratoga Springs and none with his same middle initial. It wasn't until sometime Wednesday morning I had the idea to call my cell phone provider and ask them to connect me with the last caller from the night before. They were not terribly cooperative.

I was really tired from the stress and driving. As we entered Nebraska, I started to look for a place to nap. We pulled into a rest stop before dawn and slept for about two hours. I was just as fatigued as before the rest, but Drummer was invigorated. He had not slept either. While I was driving, he was panting almost non-stop. When we approached Wyoming, I was the one who was re-energized. The first thing that hit me climbing the mountains was how difficult the trek must have been for the pioneers, especially those with the handcarts. I never appreciated the depth of their determination or conviction until I understood the physical demands imposed on them.

We stopped at no less than five motels in Wyoming: none of which would take dogs. I need to mention that Drummer was better behaved than most children. Ultimately, we arrived at the Holiday Inn in Laramie. Well worth the cost.

After a shower and meal, I settled in to email Will my whereabouts and phone number. He called, was upbeat and chatty, and waiting for our arrival the following day. I was told to take my time, assuming he was concerned about my challenges. But I felt I needed to get there for the appointment at the oncology clinic, get our marriage license, and then make it to the courts while they were still open. I was not going to jeopardize my future by staying in the same house as he, unless we were married: even if it meant another night in a motel which by then I could barely afford.

We approached the Salt Lake Valley and I was mesmerized. If ever anyone denies the hand of God in the beauty of the world, let them stand atop the approach and look down. A sense of history must overtake any LDS visitor at least the first time. I was seeing the same sight, albeit not in its virgin state, witnessed by Brother Brigham. The steep climbs and rapid descents must have been agonizing for the settlers. It was painful for me too since I was stuck behind some travelers who might as well have been driving oxen or mule teams.

New converts are usually counseled, and it was no different for me, with the traditional warnings about the adversary. I was intimately aware of its truth. Nothing that first year went easy, including the start to my new life. Even the electronics were conspiring against me. Driving in to SLC I had my GPS set for the Saratoga Springs address Will gave me. I took the precaution of checking the directions online and familiarized myself with the major turns. I had trust issues with the positioning device, having been directed too often down non-existent roads, and turns into a river. It was then the blasted thing lost the signal. I drove right by the major intersection because my GPS did not warn me. I looked at the thing with malice in my heart and found it was low on batteries. Batteries? It was plugged in! Why would it need batteries? I pulled off as soon as I could, and found batteries.

I arrived at the house not without some more stress, early Thursday afternoon. In the driveway was a clunker. Will came out to meet us and I had a sinking feeling already. It was not his looks; but more like his demeanor and body language. My fiancé was wearing a 6 gallon hat to walk out the door. Cute. We went inside where I explored the tri-level townhome. It was sparsely furnished, to say the least. However, I knew he had recently moved in and it needed furniture.

The only furnishings were a small wood veneer table and two matching chairs in the kitchen area. Downstairs was a sliding glass door leading to a very small yard; about ten feet lower than the running path next to a canal. There was a television, recliner, and cheap metal futon couch as furnishings. Upstairs on the third level, were three bedrooms. One was a master with a full bathroom and one queen sized bed, accompanied by two tray tables, and one low-wattage lamp. There were no shelves in the closet and my clothes were later sorted into baskets. The second room contained William's desktop computer and two small desks with chairs. One desk was for a student, which he offered to me. I declined and said I would use my laptop downstairs and sit in the recliner. The third room was empty except for some of Will's clothes. That was where he dressed: Definitely bizarre. Finally, there was another full bathroom in the hall, which William claimed as his. It was getting stranger by the moment.

My first priority was making sure his illness was addressed. I was incredulous when told he still had not made the call to the oncologist. I drove at breakneck speeds to reach Utah in time for an expected doctor visit. My demeanor was not that of a meek saint. I dialed the clinic without saying a word and spoke to the intake coordinator. It was no surprise his records were needed before the appointment could be made. I was annoyed and confused that he had delayed. I handed Will the phone which he took out of the room, into the hallway. There were obviously some questions asked of him and I was startled when I overheard what was apparently a reply to what kind of caner he had. William haltingly said it was colon cancer.

He told me it was prostate cancer. I assumed he was nervous and confused, so quickly corrected him. He told them he would contact his physician's office and have the documents sent. I chalked off the error but had a bad feeling. Having worked with cancer patients, I knew while many are stoic, none have ever been so unaffected by the diagnosis so soon after receiving it. There were no questions, focus on finding treatments, etc. More concerning, what doctor calls his patient with a terminal diagnosis, especially after one or two visits? When I asked about the results of his PSA, MRI, bone scan and others, William did not have any answers. With that on my mind, we headed into Provo.

I need to make it clear that by then I already knew this was definitely not the man I wanted to marry, but I had no choice. I spent just about everything I had to drive out. Gas prices were up to over $4/gallon. There were severe misgivings, but nowhere else to go. I did not know anyone to put me up, and living in the car, in August, with my dog and clothing was not a viable option. For sure I was not going to be staying in that house without a marriage. I could already anticipate what would be said if we were not wed: let alone the legal implications if this basket case decided to throw me out.

We made it to the county clerk's office and obtained the license. Patrons were given a list of places and people to contact for the actual marriage. The whole afternoon and trip was becoming surreal, especially when he told me that once you have a license in Utah you are considered married. I thought he was joking and directed him to the nearby court house. I was getting married but it felt like I had a gun to my head. He suckered me out there, what else would he be capable of? It was getting late, but we found some very cooperative people who helped us not only find a willing judge, but also witnesses. Again, I tried to forget the bad feeling and see if we could make it work.

After the ceremony I needed to stop at Wal-Mart for dog food. As we passed the jewelry counter, I was reminded of a discussion we had a few weeks before about wedding bands. I had offered to buy them but he said we would get them together. On our wedding day he said he did not want to wear one; did I? It was getting more peculiar as the day progressed. Why would you not want to wear a token of your commitment for all to see? I was not thrilled at the prospect of titanium rings, nor a purchase of something so important from the discount giant; but Will bought the cheapest wedding bands available promising better in the future. Dread came over me as I worried if I was too materialistic to expect something better. I had a sinking feeling when he announced our wedding dinner was to be at Arctic Circle. For those unfamiliar with Utah, it is the equivalent of Dairy Queen meets McDonalds.

It was a period of transition. It was disturbing he was not financially stable, and had been less than forthright with the truth. I was quite open from the beginning of our courtship regarding how and why my financial resources were non-existent for the time being. Among the subjects we discussed, and I wrote extensive emails on, was the state of my health and how I needed health insurance. I could pay for that, but in Utah only group insurance would accept me. I told him up front that I could not move to be with him unless he joined the local Chamber of Commerce, and he said he would take care of it.

We had a discussion on the way home that included questions about the Chamber of Commerce, the cost of joining and of their health insurance coverage. Will evaded the issue and talked about life insurance: and it became obsessive. I interrupted, pointing out neither of us were eligible since I had pre-existing disease, while he now had cancer. He reacted with shock and anger, as his countenance became dark. I couldn't figure out why life insurance was so important to him: especially mine. Then he informed me he had nothing. His so-called business was nothing viable. He never even filed a schedule C (tax form for businesses), and

I realized he could not have joined the Chamber. Were I to have stayed, I could have joined: but everything takes time I did not have or want to waste.

According to the story, his wife was psychotic and had cleaned him out including investments, car and homes. He was allegedly told by her psychiatrist that he should get out of the marriage at any cost. Now it was my turn to be shocked. I knew the house was sparsely furnished because he informed me it was my responsibility to furnish. At the time he said it, I didn't think it meant I would have to pay for the items myself.

Getting back to the house I took inventory of what was needed. There were a total of 4 plates and lots of recycled plastic dishes in the dishwasher. The utensils were so poor that when I cut into the loaf of homemade bread I brought with me, the knife bent. It soon became evident Will did not have a dime in spite of a decent retirement income and the part-time teaching at a community college. I suddenly understood and recognized the reason he was so insistent on marrying me. It had nothing to do with love or affection. It was purely a means to an end. He was after non-existent wealth and my writing ability. This debacle, I soon learned, was because he never read any email beyond the subject line. If he had, then the man would not have been courting me, and then driving me around that first day to look at newly built retirement communities. He thought my fantasy wealth would be spent on him.

The following morning (Friday) I called the oncologist's office, only to learn the records were never sent. Will's stated doctor's name who they said was not a urologist: or anyone they ever heard of. I asked Will to call his physician and tell them we were coming over for the records. A few minutes later he came back to explain there was a message on his voicemail that the diagnosis was for another William Richards and the office realized it when the records were requested. I knew that was a load of manure. As I said before, when I lost my phone I tried locating William Richards and there were none in the area. What is more, no physician calls a patient they are unfamiliar with to tell them they have three months to live: let alone leaves a message on voice mail apologizing for that kind of mistake. I finally conceded to myself that he had not gone to a doctor at all. I did not say anything about that to him at the time.

The state of his bank account or lack of it was more than a simple error in its telling. When I faced the reptile with his fiscal ruse, he emailed me an apology (!) stating he did a dumb thing, as well as excusing his behavior with the now familiar saga of how he had savings, money in the bank and two houses (one in South Carolina) that were ripped away from him in his divorce. I asked what happened to his lawyer and he said he didn't have one. It didn't make sense. It also was illogical that he would own a home in South Carolina since he knew nothing about the state (a place I had lived). Even more irrational was why he had no attorney.

That same afternoon I was still mulling over the morning events when we went to his UPS Store mail box and retrieved not only his new cell phone that I ordered, but the one replacing that which I lost. I said I would activate his as soon as he put the old one in the box and it was ready to ship off to the former Mrs. Richards. My mother raised one fool and it wasn't me, although my recent actions could not prove it. He hesitated and dragged his feet: something that did not make sense.

After a few days I noticed the land line never rang. When I asked, he explained that too was not in his name and the calls were never for him. Why would they be for her in this house, if she had a home of her own? I asked about paying the utilities and he replied that he hadn't checked the mail that came to the house mail box, down the street. Who lives in a house for two months and doesn't know what their gas and electric are? The stories were too inconsistent. I wondered if anything he said was true. William reported his ex-had signed the lease with him and put the utilities and TV in her name as well. It didn't add up and I told him he had to have everything changed to his name: I wasn't going to rely on his ex-wife for our responsibilities, nor should she bear the burden; crazy or not. I also quickly decided my name would go on nothing.

Because my former bishop was going to be in Utah for his daughter's wedding, I originally asked William to arrange for a church marriage in the meeting house with my former bishop and the new one. He told me everything was set, he was waiting for the Heritage Hills bishop to call him back. That went on for several weeks prior to my arrival. Will proudly informed me he introduced himself to the congregation, and announced he was soon to be married. The following Sunday I called him and had to leave a message. He called me back late, saying he had a meeting at the church. So, as we got ready for sacrament on our first Sabbath, I was anxious to meet the people he knew.

Transplanting to Utah is quite a culture shock for someone from the mission field. To be able to see the tops of three meeting houses and a stake center from your window is impressive enough; but the meeting houses are as large as our stake centers here in the east.

We came early and sat down near the side door. People came to greet us and I was stunned when someone asked if we had been to that meeting house before: Will promptly stated it was his first time. The man was an inveterate liar with a bad memory to boot. It was no wonder the issue about being married by the bishops was dropped: he never mentioned it because the bishop did not have a clue who he was. So, where was he when he was allegedly at those church meetings on Sunday evenings? It occurred to me that strangling him in his high priest white shirt before other members might have been justifiable homicide, but would not sit well when it came time for a temple recommend. I said little the rest of the day, though we did go for a walk along the canal with Drummer.

Sunday school and Relief Society were also an adventure. Going to the three hour block was like moving from a horse and wagon to a Formula 1 race car. I'd say Sunday school numbered about the same total of people who attend sacrament in my home ward. Perhaps it was the ward culture, but the way they vied to respond to the teacher and each other seemed to liken unto a blood sport. Each member appeared to be trying to outdo each other with their knowledge and memory of what leaders have said about the text, and freely quoted scripture. Amusingly, they did not have a class for neophytes like me. It was as if taking a primary child and putting them in Institute. In RS it got even bolder because with just the sisters, the gloves came off: it was like a scripture chase. The cut-throat competition was impressive and definitely struck terror in my heart. It was not exactly my speed or style. I am fortunate when I remember which chapter I am reading.

The following morning I was told we had to ride over to American Fork to deliver his rent check; he could not mail it because it was two weeks late. My husband came up with some excuse for the late payment: but obviously it was not the first time. The extent of his lies was becoming crystal clear and the reason nothing was in his name.

We had a serious discussion about his persistent lying that evening, especially when I realized he was not going to reimburse me for my expenses as he vowed. I was not going to be able to pay for health insurance, nor my car insurance, and could not afford lapsed coverage for either. He apologized but it did not seem to faze him. I had been forthright early on about my lack of resources and the nature of freelance writing, but he said he could support us with his income. It was futile: he did not even have the money for the newspaper to be delivered. I needed him to pay my car insurance that month, which he agreed to, as I paid online with his checking account. I was trapped in Utah until my delayed check was ready; which could be days or weeks. To make matters even worse, the company was becoming quite unreliable. I worked for them knowing they were members and believed they had to be inherently honest. This was another misperception of a new convert that came back to bite me. The CFO was stake YM president. I did not realize at the time there are dishonest businessmen in every faith: LDS being no exception. I was beginning to understand I was confusing the church with the people. Unfortunately, the members are not always what we would expect them to be.

I was going to try to get my not-so-loving spouse productive. Will and I talked about his seminar business: but he did not want to go on the road. William just wanted to write his books (meaning me), get an agent, and land on the best seller list. As I began to try to gain a concrete knowledge about this seminar thing, it became starkly clear that his plan was a pipe dream. How can you write a book on leadership if you are not a leader? He was a rank and file employee five years before, and there was no name recognition in that. He did not even show up on the radar with a Google search. The depth of his troubles (and now mine) stemmed from his being out of touch with reality. William truly believed he was a well-known guru and worth the $2000 a day that no one wanted to pay him.

He lived in a fantasy world. The more he talked to me about how great he was, the more I came to acknowledge he was clearly nuts.

I thought I would give it a try, since we were married, at least for the time being. I built a decent web site for him, but I was not willing to expend one more time on his behalf. He was upset that I put the burden of responsibility on him to pay for hosting, as I gave him links of inexpensive vendors.

The leadership book was a no-brainer: he was no leader and I do not write fiction. The idea for the accounting books might have worked, but all he could offer me as resource material were old workbooks. Alone, they might as well have been wallpaper. I needed to hear his lecture or read his notes to do the content. He was unprepared for that. The bare bone fact is that William W. Richards had no credentials, no notes, and no clue.

His plans also consisted of starting an MBA from some unknown school, publishing his work, and getting a job at BYU. At 67 with the inability to remember even his lies, that was highly unlikely. Being unable to focus on anything made it a surety that his plans were unrealistic. I knew no matter how hard I worked on the marriage and to forgive him, William would always be a sociopath and inveterate liar.

What love I may have had quickly turned to pain and perhaps even hatred at being used, anger at myself for falling into a trap, and unadulterated rage at his deception. I had to get out before he dragged me into his cesspool and I permanently lost the Holy Spirit with my growing revulsion.

I unexpected received an email Tuesday afternoon, asking if the late check should be sent to New York or Saratoga Springs. Fortunately, the content company was located in Sandy. I opted to take Drummer for a drive and pick it up. The Lord was looking out for me and I knew it. I retrieved the money and had my cash for the trip back. I would not be stuck with William indefinitely. Reason told me it was clearly not wise to tell the sociopath I had a significant sum in my possession.

I also was not going to tell Will I was leaving until I had my foot out the door. While I did start to be more cautious after his outburst regarding life insurance, William was probably not dangerous: despite what he would have liked me to think. However, I was not looking for contention or confrontation. Things were bad enough. He was no intellectual and was easy to predict. However, I was sure if he became physically aggressive, my dog would cripple or kill him.

The chronic liar initially told me he was in the Marine Corps Reserves for six months, and was a trained killer. I tried not to laugh. I was in the Army and knew no one taught stealth killing techniques to raw reservists like him who were trained to be clerks. I was an undergraduate physical education major who took private lessons in the martial arts. I worked in some of the toughest neighborhoods of New York City and Newark, New Jersey. I student taught in Bedford-Stuyvesant, during the riots, and the 6th graders were more dangerous than my sociopath. William posed no physical threat to me. However, I wasn't looking to create a problem.

There was one obstacle to leaving that day. The packages I brought for the newlyweds were still in the back of my SUV. My friends were tied up until Friday. Those were long days for me. I spent it doing my wash and quietly packing some items while he was out.

William was told after that incident at church that one more lie and we were through. Of course he was a liar by nature and the nonsense continued. The stories were all about him being victimized. As I watched his lips move I had a strong impulse to stuff something in his mouth to stop the litany. If all the lies were not enough, William told me early on that he had a solution to our financial problems: I give up writing and find a "real" job. He decided I should go to work as a secretary or file clerk, and sent me email links for those positions, while he was sending out resumes to be a telemarketer at $8 an hour. He was determined I would be financially productive, and provide for my own insurance needs as well. I did not need to be married to him to support myself, as well as whatever he was spending his money on. That, by the way, was the big question. I never smelled alcohol, nor saw signs of drug abuse: though both were possibilities on my mind.

I've often said there's nothing lonelier than not having a companion in a marriage. Life as a single suddenly did not look so bad any more. I made dinner every night, did the dishes, such that there were, and we each went our separate ways within the house, other than when he wanted to watch television downstairs. During that waiting period, there was little conversation between us. I was indeed angry, not trusting him at all. It did not take great insight to know he was not who I thought, and was always scheming.

One of his peculiar habits made me wonder what I was missing. It was his responsibility to do the grocery shopping. He went shopping every day, never invited me to go with him, and never bought more than what we needed for one night. The only foods he stocked up on were hot dogs and processed hash browns. Rather odd for someone claiming to be a vegan into natural foods only. In addition, Will would take a shower and be out of the house by 6 AM to be at the gym in a jogging suit. I found it weird that he showered first as well as came and went in the same outfit. He carried a gym bag with him, and other than when it was in his hand, I have no idea where he kept it. Why would you carry a bag if you did not bring a change of clothes? I never did know what was in it.

On the last Friday morning, I told William I was taking Drummer with me to drop off the wedding presents. He never asked to join us, meet my friends, or even to be in my company. When I got to the destination, I shared my experience and told them my plans to return.

I took the dog with me whenever leaving the house. I wasn't sure how much he liked Drummer, but knew Will was afraid of him; often mentioning how strong he was. He offered to take the dog for a ride, but I declined. Aside from him not asking me if I wanted to go, it was too out of character. I could imagine him letting the pooch out to die of heat stroke, or harming him and claiming he was attacked. I wanted him to fear my 4 footed companion: and I did nothing to dispel the notion of the dog being dangerous.

When we got back to the house I informed William we were done. He had jeopardized my life, forced me to expend funds I did not have, bear the burden of repaying what he in effect borrowed, and he consistently lied. He did not take the news badly; in fact he seemed relieved as he helped me move my clothes out to the car.

On one trip through the garage, I walked over to where I thought he was putting my stuff, only to find my bag was much heavier than I recalled packing. I looked again and realized that particular red bag on wheels was not mine. It was then a light bulb went off in my mind: that was his suitcase! Will was getting ready to abandon me alone in that leased house, and take off on his own! My loving husband was planning on leaving me without a dime, in a house where the utilities would probably be shut off in a matter of days, and with nothing to eat.

I could not get out of there fast enough. I knew the Lord was with me.

The trip back was less stressful than on the way out. Imagine what goes through your mind after an experience like William. My friends thought me crazy and rash to marry so quickly. So did I: sometimes risks pay off, not that my track record would prove it. I do not know why I thought that, since I had never won at casinos, lottery or even bingo. Perhaps my years outside the church gave me a different perspective. However, that triggered more thoughts. Should I return to my ward? Despite the admonition to nurture new members, that message was only absorbed by a few. I knew there were some who were not pleased with my lack of being, shall we call it, demur? As I said earlier, I do not play games. I earned every one of my grey hairs and will not pretend to be anything less than I am. This little fiasco would certainly set their tongues wagging and be fodder for many. I decided to do what I had to do. I joined the church because it is true, and not for the social life. I go to sacrament meetings because of obedience, and take the sacrament to sustain me. I don't care what anyone thinks: anyone.

When I returned to my ward after a two week hiatus, there was no lack of comments to my face or behind my back. It was harder walking in those doors after six months than the first time I set foot in the place.

That I married an alleged high priest with a temple recommend doesn't mean the church is to blame; only the people who knew of his predilection for lying and left it for someone else to deal with. I have no idea whether his previous bishops or branch presidents knew about his lifestyle, but find it hard to believe they did not.

My personal thoughts on the matter are that God chooses the prophet and hierarchy. I think that sometimes, on the local levels, the Lord lets inequities happen for a reason: leaders are called for different motives or just expediency. Perhaps some bishops are selected by the Lord, knowing they will fail, and to teach the saints a lesson or test their faith: or to provide a lesson for the one called. I was not in the church six months when everything I trusted appeared to be disintegrating before my eyes. It was just the beginning of my test and I had to keep reminding myself of something said by a friend, way back in Vermont: the church is perfect; it is the people who are not.

I wanted an annulment but soon found that no lawyer would take the case without at least $600 up front, then fees and court costs. Who had that amount after my adventure? I did learn the State of Utah has a do-it-yourself divorce for $200, and I would not need an attorney for that. What's more, if I could not afford it then they would collect the fee from him. That sounded good to me. Getting Will's social security number and birth date, however, was proving to be a challenge; he didn't answer my emails or phone calls. When he finally did, he said he had been in Mexico, away from his computer, training for a possible position. It was as absurd as it sounds.

On the day I mailed my divorce papers to the court, GEICO sent notice that my auto policy was being cancelled for non-payment. The check from Will's account was rejected as being unauthorized. I emailed him and he said he would pay it. The reptile claimed he did not recognize what it was for and stopped payment. Will knew what the check to GEICO was: I watched him write it in his check register. He also suddenly inquired about the paper work for the divorce.

The Rest of the Story

The following morning I received a call from someone who introduced herself as Connie. She had all the missing pieces to the puzzle called William Richards.

Before starting up with me, he was going to marry her and she was the one who sparsely furnished the house; not his ex. She moved out days before he contacted me.

The week before I went out there, Will was still trying to reconcile with her. She met him on the same dating site I did. Connie flew to Utah to meet with him, as well as visit with her children and grandchildren. They agreed to lease a house together and live platonically to see if they were compatible. Over the course of a month or slightly more, she left him twice because of his violent outbursts. The second time she went home to South Carolina.

Remember that cell phone that his ex-wife allegedly paid for? It was Connie's contract. The vermin told her all the phone calls to me were made to a dying friend of his mother. Connie and William were still in communication all through our marriage. He attempted reconciliation, professing his love, and longing to be with her: this was going on all the time we were married. He never mentioned that minor detail to either of us. The day I left for Utah he wrote her asking how they would arrange to get back together: would she come to Utah or he to South Carolina? While crawling into bed with me at night, he was writing love letters to her during the day.

He talked her into reconciliation. The man moved to South Carolina with the help of her grandson; to stay in her house and marry in a few weeks. She discovered his lies when she saw the certified mail copy of our marriage certificate, which he inadvertently handed her with the rest of the forwarded mail. Brother Richards was going to marry her before being served by me with divorce papers and not tell her he was even married.

Connie learned from looking at his bank statement that Will was spending $1000/month on alcohol. Initially, he told her I was the drinker and spending the money. He said I just showed up at the door one day and demanded we get married. That would come under the heading of totally impossible. The only address I had for him was the one on the bottom of his emails: which was the UPS Store. He gave me the house address the night before I left for Happy Valley.

William has methodically abdicated any financial responsibility. He always had his spouse handle his checking account and later accused them of manipulation. Fortunately, I told him I would have no part of handling his money.

So the good high priest was communicating with a girlfriend while courting and married to me; was not going to wait for the divorce to marry again; and best of all, told me to serve him at an address he had moved away from (which also left Connie responsible for the $1100 a month lease). That nonsense about being out of the country to train for a potential job was as much of a lie as his other flights of the imagination: he was driving to South Carolina.

Connie too had put out money on his behalf. When he arrived in South Carolina he gave her a check for $1000. After she threw him out, Will called to tell her he was stopping the check because he needed money to live on. It was a message on her voice mail. The phone he called from was in a local motel.

I received an email that day from him indicating he would pay me back $200 a month once he was settled. I wasn't sure I could believe him, and rightfully so.

Connie was the key to everything, and gave me contact information for Millie: his real ex-wife. I had the opportunity to talk to Millie:

who had just signed her divorce affidavit the week I filed. He married me while knowingly still wed to her; and the worthy priesthood holder was going to marry Connie as well! It came as no surprise that Millie is one of the sweetest and most stable people I know, despite having lived with Will for two years. She was terrified of him because of his threats and violent outbursts. When she separated from him, Will found a spot in a public area and cut his foot just enough to bleed profusely, but not die. This was his bid for attention with a pathetic pseudo suicide. Why suicide? Because it was a way to get back at Millie, knowing her first husband and real love suffered from severe depression; in the end taking his own life. Will thought he knew what the guilt would do to her; but it did not. From Millie we all learned much about Will's inappropriate behavior, constant lies, and abusive language. She learned late he was an alcoholic. He mentioned life insurance to her as well. He was irate when Millie said she would take it out for herself: and name her grandchildren as beneficiaries.

From Millie I received the email address of his previous wife, to whom he married and divorced twice. Millie knew some of the alleged history, but never had contact with the woman. The sister responded to me that she was married to him about 20 years. William told Connie they were divorced because she got fat.

Nice guy that he is to be proud of that. The truth is that she demanded the divorce because he was drinking and playing around with other women. Had she reported him to her bishop, the rest of us may have gotten away unscathed and Will would have had to find a different theater for his dramas. As for my confusion, it was because I received the convoluted version of his previous marriages by his combining all his women into one person.

I learned in South Carolina and Utah there is little to be done to remove a threat to women such as Will Richards. After speaking to a number of state and local Utah offices, I landed in the Provo detective bureau. They do not make it easy. First, they insist you come in to file the report in person. They did not see me as the offended party, rather Millie. If I wanted to file then I would have to be in court for every appearance, and the defendant can postpone the proceedings indefinitely even the day of the scheduled appearance. Without the plaintiff, the judge can and will throw the case out. That would mean having to drive or fly to Utah every time a hearing was slated. It did not matter what evidence there was. Furthermore, since he was living out of state, they had no jurisdiction to arrest him. South Carolina said it did not happen in their state so there is nothing they could do. It seems the system is more anxious to protect the rights of predators than victims.

Some emails received by Millie and myself indicated William was headed back to Utah. We thought there had to be a way to stop him from doing further damage to LDS sisters. On behalf of the three of us I wrote a letter to the Relief Society President, asking for a contact list of RS presidents to warn them of the danger. It was a naïve thing to do but we were concerned. They rushed into action at glacial speeds. Three months later someone from church security called my bishop to ask if I was in danger. You can draw your own conclusions on how serious the church took the situation at that time. Millie, however, remains terrified of Will; certain she will meet her maker by William's hand. Although she has an order of protection, and has moved, he has found ways to torment her.

Connie started gathering all her information regarding a harassment charge for his multiple nasty phone calls and intimidating emails. Will was warned by the local police to have no contact with her. Connie, Millie, nor I responded to his email or phone calls. It gave Will no one to manipulate and undoubtedly frustrated him. He was sending Connie and me similar emails, unaware the three of us knew each other and what he was up to. Some notes made no sense. He claimed to Connie he quit drinking. Hard to believe he had the will to go cold turkey. In an effort to keep track of him I was sometimes civil and often brazen in telling him about his inadequacies. Just about that time a neighbor of Connie's noticed Will parked near her house. Friday of the following week a court issued a warrant for his arrest. They added stalking to the charges of harassment and set the bail at $30,000. He did not have the $3000 for the bondsman, and apparently tried to contact Millie but she did not answer the call.

One morning I received a call from the Saluda County Detention Center. They had his cell phone (which he denied having to the judge) and called me since my number was listed on it. Will was acting confused when they brought him up front to use the land line. There was a question whether he had Alzheimer's. I told them he was probably going into alcoholic withdrawal, and gave them Connie's number. She spent more time talking to them. He told them he wanted to transfer money between accounts but they would not leave him alone so he acted confused. He was trying to make a phone call to someone, she guesses, but did not want them to listen in. I doubt too it was to transfer money, since he probably did not have any. She told them a lot more than they ever wanted to know, I am sure.

Will went into the hospital following that episode, but they discharged him the following weekend because they did not want to pay for a deputy to sit with him waiting to recover from his DTs. As soon as he was released he conned a neighbor into taking him to the liquor store saying his aunt needed it. There was a hearing a few days later and a plea agreement was accepted. The sentence was probation since he has no other record (bigamy obviously doesn't count). They offered him the option to leave the state, I think after paying fines and restitution, but he said he would stay. It would have been tough to leave since the auto lender contacted Connie and she told them where they could repossess his car which was 3 months behind. Somehow he was able to rent cars for a while and apparently obtained one permanently.

Ultimately William's temple recommend was physically retrieved. I learned it was actually revoked when he was married to Millie, and the bishop did not buy his story about why he wasn't tithing. He asked for the card back but never pursued the matter. Had he done so, Will would not have been able to produce the card when I asked about it or Connie did. At the time the bishop also did not know Will got drunk the night before going to the temple. His status as a high priest was not questioned by the bishop even though the church records from Texas never indicated so. Will told the bishop the document must be lost.

In the meanwhile, Will ingratiated himself to his new branch president. The man, by chance, also happened to be Connie's home teacher. By then, she had started dating her ex-husband, and living in a guest house on his property. President Redneck had the nerve to ask Victor if he would pick up William on his way to church on Sunday. His response was "hell, no!" The branch president told Connie and Victor they will have to find a new place to worship since William was attending theirs, and a court order prevented him from coming within 100 feet of her. Additionally, though, when Connie, Millie, and I gave witness to all William has done and lied about, the leader chose to believe the reptile and befriended him. William sat with the president's family to take weekly sacrament.

Will told the brother I had traveled the 2200 miles to his house uninvited, and forced him into marriage. According to what the branch president told my bishop, I just showed up at his door one day despite his telling me not to come. He added that I was an alcoholic and married for his money. He said he did not know his divorce from Millie was not final, claiming unfamiliarity with the divorce process despite three previous ones. That he was going to marry Connie while knowingly married to me, counted for nothing in President Redneck's eyes.

I had presented President Redneck with the incriminating emails between Will and Connie sent during our marriage (provided willingly by her). Fidelity was not an issue to the branch president. Connie bore witness of the things Will had done to her, as did Millie; whose testimony was the most damning of all. All this and that Will had written those love letters while wed to me, was excusable since he was a drunk; which none of us knew until after the fact. Will was being victimized and much maligned said the local leadership. He was told to repent, go to AA, and that was the end of it. The appointed leader and the stake president jointly found no reason for disciplinary action.

If ever there was a time I had a test of faith that was it. In the witness of three these men determined we were hysterical women whose testimonies counted for absolutely nothing. They obviously were absent or not paying attention at some of the General Conference priesthood broadcasts discussing the treatment of sisters. However, these men made their own rules. Connie told me they would do nothing before we started, and I did not believe her: surely these brethren would forsake their stereotypes as characters out of the movie "Deliverance". I was sure right makes might and they would suspend the old redneck mentality, to protect their church and sisters. I was wrong.

It didn't end there. I would not let go. I wrote a letter to the branch president expressing my outrage and disappointment with his apparent disregard for the three of us. I ended with a quote from Isaiah

5.20 - 23:

Woe unto them that call evil good, and good evil; that put darkness for light, and light for darkness; that put bitter for sweet, and sweet for bitter

Woe unto them that are wise in their own eyes, and prudent in their own sight!

Woe unto them that are mighty to drink wine, and men of strength to mingle strong drink:

Which justify the wicked for reward, and take away the righteousness of the righteous from him!

That instigated a note from my bishop, berating me like a child. He insultingly said: "I only know your side of the story" and while he supported the initial efforts, believed it should rest after the decision was made. I was castigated for criticizing a judge of Israel who bears tremendous responsibility in a non-paying position. It was a good test of my ability to manage my temper and words. I found his comments lame, having put in plenty of time in volunteer positions before ever hearing of the church, and thought that was a poor response considering the man is supposed to be engaged in the work of the Lord. There was a veiled threat that when one goes to the temple we covenant not to criticize. My response was that I was not yet endowed and would say what I want. Just for the record, speaking evil is a whole lot different than criticizing.

After I cooled off some, I learned the meaning of heartfelt prayer. Before I started, my inclination was to beg the Lord to wipe them all off the face of the earth, but first have all their teeth fall out except one; and that one to require root canal without anesthesia. Impotence and bad breath would just be the icing on the cake. However, I found myself asking that the hate, anger, and malice be removed from my heart. Slowly, but faster than I expected, that all came to pass. In the end, I know it will be Jesus who will decide the fate of those who dismissed all we said. Unfortunately, as a recent church essay confirms, all too often women's concerns are dismissed on the local levels.

Even after the counseling he received to leave the three of us alone, the vicious and nonsensical email notes continued. William again promised his branch president he would stop writing me, when I complained about his hate mail. In spite of what the brother told him, he continued. The result was that the president washed his hands of William and told my bishop

111

to have me block him or take legal action. They decided there will be no church intervention since the man is beyond help. Yet, he remained a high priest to the parade of ecclesiastic leaders in his miserable life.

I received a call in May of that year, from a Lexington County Probation Officer: William skipped town in violation of his court order and there was an arrest warrant issued for his return. He told his landlord he was going to live with his daughter, and Lorenzo asked me if I knew where that was. I was still irate with all that happened and it gave me a great sense of purpose to share what I knew: and it was a lot. I saved almost all correspondence from the reptile and figured out the address of his daughter in West Jordan. William, in a moment of trying to demonstrate that someone cared for him, shared a letter from her some months before. In it she welcomed his contact after so many years and described in significant detail where she lived, as well as information about her husband.

To digress for a moment, I'm quite certain she was unaware her private details were going out to others. We all knew they had been estranged for a number of years, and wondered what he was up to. I took the liberty of writing to her with details of Will's life she should know about. Although there was no reply, the young woman had fair warning of what her father was like before he ever jumped probation. I do not fault her for being loyal. It is her blood and only living relative. She showed Christian compassion and even obtained the services of an attorney for him. However, you can be kind and loving to an asp but it will still bite you when it gets the opportunity.

I gave Connie, who was temporarily in Utah for the summer, the information. She drove past and identified his car in his daughter's driveway. Connie then went to the West Jordan Police. However, the warrant did not extend to extradition from Utah. No one would pick him up.

South Carolina stated it did not have the money to retrieve him and it would cost more than the amount he owed them and his bounced $1000 check. Moral of the story is that if you commit a crime in South Carolina that is not heinous (I am assuming their standard for heinous is similar to more sophisticated states) and escape outside its borders, you are home free.

William, however, may have escaped the law, but not justice. His daughter and her spouse were solid Mormons and there was no question that his records would be transferred to their ward. Apparently the branch president in South Carolina probably gave a sigh of relief and perhaps a slight change of heart (not that he did anything about it when he realized his error in judgment, or apologized to any of us for his insulting and demeaning behavior). Among the information shared with the new bishop were all of our emails regarding Will's antics. I suspect, given the wealth of content sent, President Redneck was glad to be relieved of living with his mistakes.

Will's daughter and son-in-law had a bishop who, there is no doubt in my mind, received revelation and inspiration. He was distressed when he had the opportunity to look through what must have been a voluminous file. He then spoke with everyone involved, including his new congregant, and determined there were enough issues to bring to the stake president and a disciplinary hearing. This judge of Israel was astute and needed no assistance from any mortal to discern the lies from reality.

An example shared with Connie and I was when the bishop was sitting on the platform the first fast and testimony day William attended. The Spirit prompted the bishop that Will would get into the testimony line, and the bishop was to escort William into the hall, explaining it was inappropriate at the time. Sure enough, Will got into line and the bishop got off the platform.

Just before the disciplinary hearing, Will was asked to leave his daughter's home, after the family council met and agreed. He disappeared for a few months and reappeared again. The bishop and high council took no time in convening a hearing. It is my understanding they never even mentioned the reptile's abuse of we three; that they had enough other matters, including his illegal flight, to excommunicate him. That means he will have to pay restitution should he ever want to come back. Knowing Will, he is somewhere pretending to be a member but will never be back. His repentance in either matter is unlikely.

Connie and I received a note from the bishop in Utah, stating that Will's son-in-law met with him for a while one day, discussing some of the activities occurring in their home. The bishop shared some information and thoughts from his investigation, observation, and intervention regarding William. That evening, while Will was out of the house, Mark, Cathy, and the children voted William out of the house. When Will returned, Mark invited him to leave immediately.

Just about the time that occurred, the stake president was planning on a meeting with William to schedule a stake disciplinary hearing. Upon learning Will went under the radar, the stake president notified the church welfare system fraud hotline and registered his name, with instructions to contact the official if and when Will appears. The church records for William Richards were sent to church headquarters and the "address unknown" file, with a similar note. Within a few months Will contacted his daughter to tell her he was evicted from his apartment. It was Christmas season and they issued a temporary invitation to return. That was enough for the stake presidency to take action. The man who made his own rules is no longer associated with the church. Our statements were not necessary since there was enough to be said about his conduct excluding the sisters.

I sometimes wonder if perhaps my meeting Will didn't have a positive effect on the Lord's church. He had been a predator within the church. My odyssey may have taken time but it served a good purpose. As I told Connie, we cannot protect the women of the world from him; but we have done a valiant job bringing it to the attention of the brethren who will do their part to protect the sisters and the church.

I learned much from the experience, including how to pray diligently. Praying for Him to remove the hate and anger had results soon afterward: so much so that the reptile's name has been submitted for the prayer rolls. I have not quite reached the point where I have submitted the name of the branch president who trivialized Will's actions and outright rejected all that was reported and documented by the sisters. I do know the Lord Jesus will judge them both and it is no longer my concern. I have, however, written a note of forgiveness to the redneck; of course that has had no response either.

Back Home

My challenges did not diminish after William. Life returned to some semblance of normal and I set about my writing. The company I contracted with was, as I said earlier, located in Sandy, Utah. The CFO and CEO held stake leadership positions, so I felt comfortable that they could be trusted as the payments grew later and later. My contract stated I would be paid on the fifth of the month. When I was in Saratoga Springs, I did not receive my money until some time after the 23rd. Earlier during the summer I asked if there was a problem since it had been months since the checks came on a timely basis. The CFO denied any problems. In September, when it was late again, I pointed out if there were no problems, then I expected them to honor the terms of their contract. I was informed that the paper signed by them was merely a guideline; I would be paid after their investors, and it was none of my business if there were problems. I was informed it was rude to ask to be paid ahead of others.

After a decidedly contentious discussion I was not unexpectedly told my services would no longer be needed. I never got paid for the work of the last month, nor did most of the other writers that I know of. A few continued to provide their work with hopes of someday getting what was owed.

I talked to the CEO, who is an unpretentious brother that means well. The business suffered severe reversals and the offices had to close, in addition to full-time employees being laid off. I decided not to sue because it would do no good. Yet, it taught me a lesson about how some of the saints hold to different standards in their personal and business lives. Oddly, the CFO saw nothing wrong with his actions and somehow has determined I deserved to be disparaged because I protested and pointed it out to others after getting no answer from him.

There are many writers out there who will confirm that before undertaking any major project, you should be sure the publisher is reliable. I thought I hit the gold standard, knowing their backgrounds in the church. Another lesson learned about the wheat and the tares.

I found some gigs creating web site text. The pay was poor, but so was I. Eventually there were two problems presenting with one company in particular, also located in Utah. I never learn. The economy was in decline and less people were paying to have their sites done by professionals. Those that did use a design company were expecting miracles because they thought a website alone would bring them traffic. It did not matter they were trying to sell garbage, items that could easily be found cheaper, or even not knowing what they wanted to vend. They wanted champagne designs for beer budget prices. Yet, these clients had no idea of what they wanted and I wasted lots of unpaid time discussing ideas, only to spend sometimes weeks getting hold of them for approval. No approval, no pay. Furthermore, there was a hierarchy to getting accounts and because I was relatively new, I was stuck in the middle tier. That meant the upper tier would have first choice and cleaned out the list before I ever got to see it. If you do not have anything in your pipeline for two weeks, they fire you. Figure that one out: the top tier takes all the gigs and you get nothing. It's a little more complicated than that, but you get the idea.

My income depended on daily trolling of the writing job boards. I picked up a few projects that paid the bills; but not many.

Mormon Gold

On the brighter side, I had my temple recommend in time for my first anniversary. As luck would have it, the temple was closed for maintenance that week. So, one year from my confirmation I received my endowment, accompanied by my friends locally and Vermont.

You know though, this in no way precluded the challenges. My income was too erratic and I decided to collect early social security. One month after my birthday the check came and it was like a lifeline. However, I felt quite uneasy not being able to earn a living. Being financially devastated is degrading and depressing. I could not figure out what to do. I was working on a novel, but that was more to occupy my time than to publish. Still, writing was more for my amusement than looking for commercial success.

One morning I woke up with a strong impression I should go back into medicine. How can that be? Sure, I have a license and have been writing articles explaining medical news for lay readers; but could I pass the certifying exam again? Who would hire me after a ten year hiatus? I ordered books, started studying, and of course prayed. It did not seem to me I was absorbing all I needed to. It scared me.

In the fall of the year I was invited to an interview for a group that provides care to adult homes. It was part-time. Two days later I was hired. Again, that was not the end. I was told I had to provide my own malpractice insurance and get a DEA number (to write for controlled substances). I spent the next five days trying to figure how I would pay the nearly $2000. I could not. I was not going to borrow either, in case I got sick or something happened and I would be stuck with the debt. I got on my knees to ask the Lord what he would have me do. I initially prayed for an opportunity, and He gave it to me. I was quite prepared to just give up and try another avenue. I told my potential employer I could not take the position and explained why. He offered to pick it up for me.

The patients are those who are not sick enough for a nursing home; but are unable to care for themselves at home. It is easy to see why many people do not want to work in those kinds of environments, since such conditions make us acutely aware of our own mortality. I, however, loved it for a while. It is an opportunity to demonstrate the love of Christ for God's children, though society may have forgotten them. I will never forget my first day. Though I cannot recall what prompted my response to one patient, when I said that everyone in the home is a child of God, I do have a vivid recollection of his face. The man was overcome with emotion, thanking me as his eyes welled with tears.

I firmly believe God answers prayers. I have asked to be an instrument in his hands and to do His will. Perhaps this was one mission in life.

I spent the years since joining, wondering why the Lord would bring me to His church. What does a single, older woman without any family have to offer? Why would He take a sinner like me and make it possible for me to return to His presence? Obviously, it is not something I am likely to know the reason for in this lifetime. However, I have a persistent feeling that my paternal grandmother, who I never knew, is pleased that I have done her ordinances along with those of her family I can identify. I am at rest knowing that the friend, who I devoted all those years to and who was responsible for all my troubles, has had all her ordinances performed. The same goes for my father, who was an abusive and undoubtedly troubled man. I have learned how to forgive.

I think there are times I am like a Pharisee, but not because of some aloof aspiration. It is because I do not have that many years left in this probation and I cannot afford to err this late in the trial period. I know my weaknesses and go out of my way to avoid falling prey to them. There are people I met who have a very different interpretation of this church and its demands, as demonstrated by Ronald. I have little patience for those who go through the motions but do not read their scriptures or try to expand their knowledge. One person has even gone on a mission and does not believe Joseph was capable of revelation. That is hypocrisy. The same thing holds for a member that is unfamiliar with the concept of telling the truth at all times. What they do and how the Lord handles them is none of my business; but it is not something I am capable of handling with charity in my heart; at least not yet; so I avoid them.

The bottom line is this: I am sometimes quick-tempered, intolerant of stupidity, have little patience for nonsense, and have a hard time turning my cheek when someone has decked me. Yet, Heavenly Father has found something of value in my imperfect soul, and loves me as no other could or would. Jesus is part of my heart and soul. Nothing else matters because it can not possibly get any better than this.

A Primer for Online Dating

As I recently explained to a widow, there is nothing to be afraid of with online dating as long as you are cautious, use your brain, and respect yourself.

I tried LDS sites with little success. Lots of men sign up, not understanding what LDS means or our values. Some vendors make an effort to craft questions that mandate knowledge of the faith, but others ask the same questions as non-sectarian sites. However, there are many fools out there that have no idea what they are answering and try to pretend they are members in good standing. For instance, a common question asks if they have a current temple recommend. It is a dead giveaway when the respondent indicates "yes" and the follow-up question about church attendance says "when I get around to it" or "never". We won't even go into their response for "are you endowed?" The free sites are twice as bad. Everyone, male or female, can count on being contacted by a con artist. They are in love with you within a day or two, will send you money as long as they can get your bank account number so they can wire it, or will give you a sob story how, usually on a weekend, they were robbed at gunpoint and their bank doesn't open until Monday morning. I could go on, but that's not why you are here.

There is a lot written, said, and discussed about dating. Everyone has advice for the youngsters starting out and those under thirty who have not found their eternal companion. Since this is a tome about what I learned on my path to enlightenment, I am here to tell you the rules of search change as we get into counting decades as opposed to years. If you haven't dated in more than twenty years, you are in for culture shock. I should also say here that if you are a widow or widower, please pay attention but your circumstances may be influenced by your feelings for your deceased spouse. Who you are looking for depends on whether this next spouse will be sealed to you; or do you just want to be companions on this world? You need to be up front about your intent.

My life altering instruction from this venture demonstrated none of my long years of formal and street education were preparatory. Were the situations often not so funny they would be quite pathetic. I would like to share experiences here to accomplish several purposes:

To let those of you who are happily wed, know what being single late in life is all about

Keep others alert to navigating the nuances of senior LDS dating

Urge brothers and sisters to set the bar high enough to avoid becoming another ex

To provide some reality when considering cruising LDS dating sites

Where to Look

Let's start this discussion with some things which may or may not be evident to those new at it: just because it has "LDS" or "Mormon" in its name doesn't mean the site is monitored, run by or in any way connected to the Church of Jesus Christ of Latter Day Saints. For the most part, anyone can sign up, and do. If you go to a non-denominational site then be certain to put in your "about me" section how you feel about being Mormon and that is who you are seeking. Many non-members are unfamiliar and assume it's just another of the 6000 sects of Christianity. You will get "hits" from people who have no intention of respecting your belief in chastity (and probably little else), nor will they want to hear about it either.

For those of you not yet undergoing your social baptism by fire, here's a bit of edification. The web can be a great tool to supplement those singles events sponsored by various wards and stakes. However, you are not a child anymore but that does not mean you cannot be targeted for a scam or misled.

One Way Is To Know Who Your Potential Date Is

Don't become so bold, daring and stupid that you rush the process. I happen to believe a lot can be learned from an individual if you keep them writing for a while, before you talk. Eventually, and we're not using a time frame of hours, they and you become familiar and more comfortable. Writing removes the pressure to think fast or make quick decisions about going out. You might be surprised how those among us surrender under the weight into meeting a lot quicker when on the phone than when writing. A relationship which will last is one that is worth taking the time to invest in learning all you can.

Picking a Site to Start the Search

There are several free sites out there and at this writing three in particular for us Mormons. Avoid them like the plague, especially if you are a woman. Free is a good indication those joining want something for nothing. While it may be human nature, we are talking about the rest of your life and into the next. You get what you pay for. Rarely did I find a man who belonged to the free site as well as a paid one: but only rarely. Not that any open to the public site is REALLY secure, but no pay means they can give a pseudonym and creative information. At least with a paid service there is a credit card or Paypal account that may be traced; and at a minimum you know the person is more likely to be real. Even those gift debit cards require some identification. Not fail proof, but better than not knowing anything. Women, by the way, can be charlatans and gold diggers as easily as their counterparts. None of the free sites require proof of membership in the church. Actually, it's a problem throughout the industry (and make no mistakes: sponsors are in it for the money and not altruism). Just about all of the paid sites permit non-members and even invite them to join with incentives. I'm sure it has little to do with "every member a missionary". That's for a different discussion.

There have been lots of stories to tell. One amusing experience was a result of one of those freebees: ultimately making the user swear them off. She received a note from a "Frank" who stated in his profile he was a widower with an adolescent son, financially well off and seeking to ride into the sunset with a loving woman. He said he was an Irishman, educated in engineering at Oxford and owned a construction company here in the States. The man could barely string two sentences together with a complete thought, and let's just say it wasn't the Queen's English. She asked something about his faith after he had given a spiel about meeting and doing what Mormons don't do before marriage. He received a little lesson on the church teachings and a charitable invitation to visit LDS.org. About an hour later he was ready to convert. The new investigator was given the 800 number for information; but she was told he wanted personal instruction. Right. It didn't take long to figure something was going on; especially when he sent a list of questions like whether she owned her home, what kind of car she drove and just about everything except social security number and bank balance. She ditched him; but a few days later received a distressed email stating something "terrible" had happened to his son: robbers broke into the motel where they were living (financially secure?!), beat him up, stole his wallet and shot the kid in the arm. The boy was going to die unless he came up with $2400 to pay the doctor to remove the bullet. Could the sister please send him the funds and he promised to pay it back as soon as the banks opened and he could get access to his money?

The sister knew the whole thing was a setup from the first day. This particular incident was a "gotcha" moment. Have you ever heard of a large construction company not having health insurance for their employees? How about a U.S. hospital refusing emergency treatment and demanding cash up front? Doesn't happen.

Two days later she noticed him on another site and informed them of the idiot predator. My suspicion was that he is more like a native of a third world country who never got beyond third grade. The picture had to be bogus as well.

The sister forgot about deleting her profile until receiving a note from someone equally as literate claiming to be divorced with a young son too. When they start their letter with "Dear Sweetheart" and don't even know you, get your running shoes ready.

Not to insult your intelligence, but there are individuals of both sexes with intentions that are not exactly gospel-like. This applies to all sites, and readers are cautioned their loneliness may be hard to bear but being setup because of stupidity is heartache you REALLY don't want. Once you enter into conversation and it progresses to regular email, get smart. If it looks like you're going to hit it off, after a while of blind email correspondence and maybe even phone calls, there's another step to protect yourself. The majority of people will give you an email address from a free service (Yahoo, Gmail, Hotmail, etc.). Anyone can set those up with no confirmation. Unless they are using a computer in the public library, and don't have one of their own, get their REAL email address: and use it. If you consider going out then they need to be honest with whom they are. Phone calls are confirmation of nothing since they can be made from disposable cells. A scam artist doesn't mind spending thirty bucks to reap in your hard earned greenbacks.

There's something we need to go back to with free membership sites. Unless they belong to other paid sites, this may be a red flag for CHEAP. It could also mean they are married and don't want their spouse to know they are seeking adventure online or otherwise. Yeah: even LDS have been known to stray (excommunication not withstanding). Perhaps they merely just can't afford to pay: a factor which may be of concern to you.

Paid and Free Sites

It is recommended, if you don't already have one, get an email account with one of the free email services. Use this address in any initial correspondence with a potential partner until you are comfortable giving them your true information. It's just one more layer of protection and should you find this isn't the sister or brother of your prayers, and they won't take "no thank you", the account can be closed and they will disappear into the ether.

I joined LDS sites wanting a brother who believes the same things. If you are not so selective, or don't mind recruiting a non-member, it won't matter if you date LDS or not. However, consider that a person's conversion and commitment needs to be based on the love of the Lord; not on the basis of love for a spouse. Sure, it is a motivating factor but you will never know, will you? Without the true belief, you will have your spouse in this life: will you in the next? I am definitely NOT saying it doesn't work; just pointing out it needs to be thought about. In the Old Testament Ronnie stands as a perfect example of how love can change an individual's heart and love of the Heavenly Father.

LDS sites certainly have their advantages, but all are not equal. There are other sites open to everyone (non-sectarian) who allegedly matches you with your preferences. 'T ain't so. I stated LDS and got agnostics, atheists, Buddhists and everyone but Druids or LDS.

For the moment, this is addressing sisters and brothers who are happy with doing missionary work but not when searching for their eternal partners. Some of the Mormon websites ask questions about the applicant's relationship with the church. Be careful and read the answers. If someone states they are temple worthy and rarely attend services it should raise a flag. Could it be a simple error of clicking the wrong answer? Sure; but more likely they are lying about being temple worthy, probably not knowing what it means: not being members who are just guessing. People who don't check the boxes when available are equally suspect.

You have to set your own standards and mine may not be yours. Perhaps you are willing to work with an inactive member and bring them back to the fold. Bless you. I've done that already and now I am going to find someone who can be leaned on spiritually, and who takes his priesthood seriously.

Then there's the question put to site members, usually, about their relationship with the church. If it's blank I've learned to just keep moving by. We are taught to praise the Lord and his church. It is also something most of us want to do and do not require someone to force us. A man or woman who has no desire to define their relationship with the restored church, is going to have other flaws (and we're not choosing the wrong word either: it's one of the basic tenets and there is no such thing as "it's personal" when looking for an eternal mate).

Profiles

We all have our idea of who we want to spend eternity with. To attain that goal you need to be honest with yourself as well as the people you are trying to attract. There are legions of stories from both men and women about the pictures posted not matching the people they meet. I am reminded of a date before understanding the intricacies of this sort of sport. The guy was quite relieved when we met for lunch. I looked like my pix. Sometime earlier he met a woman who he kept staring at and finally could not contain his curiosity, when he mentioned she bore little resemblance to the picture she posted. Was it an old picture? "No" she replied. It was of her daughter but since the younger woman resembled her it was adequate to attract dates! After a few minutes of him rambling on about himself and all his toys, I had little compassion for him and his story of the overweight, over age disappointment of the story, I thought about how I didn't spend enough time getting to know him before subjecting myself to such torture. But, it somewhat shocked me that putting up an inaccurate picture was a practice at all. It's caveat emptor (buyer beware).

What can anyone possibly gain from concealing their true features? Think you're too chunky? Do you believe once the brother or sister sees you in person they will forgive and forget you lied to them? It's a heck of a way to start a relationship and my guess is it won't get beyond the first date. Pay attention to what they say in their profile; you can learn volumes about them by what is not said.

One guy from Iowa appeared to be pleasant enough but the section asking about his faith was blank or similar to "I believe". Something told me after a few conversations to get an answer. Rather than insult him I asked if he had ever been to the grove. He replied "what grove?" Ummm, "the sacred grove". He didn't know what I was referring to. I next asked how he felt about the church and he said he respected it. Now, this guy had been on the site for quite a while and would have to be an idiot not to understand it was for Mormons. If it makes no difference to you, that's fine: but it does to me and I was irritated at the charade:

but learned a lesson. His reply asked if only women could be converts. My feelings were if you want an LDS women it better be as an eternal partner and you need to be thinking baptism; not just dating. Hard line? Harsh? Perhaps but we're too old to play games and marry someone who doesn't respect you enough to understand a commitment to the Lord and his church. I don't want a temporary partner. Your thoughts may be different.

What You See Is Not Always What You Get

My advice is to avoid until you really feel secure. Most sites do not provide a mechanism to preserve your chat conversations. Emails give you the opportunity to ponder what's been said as many times as you like. Are there conflicts in the stories or did you just misunderstand? One of the predators kept urging me to use the external IM (as in AIM, Yahoo, or MSN) but because I kept his emails I was able to provide proof of his scam for the site administrators and police.

I received a note from another man claiming to be an electrical engineer who studied at Oxford and now lived in Alexandria, Virginia. A widower of 18 years with a 19 year old son in college, it sounded eerily like the illiterate who claimed to be Irish and studied at

Cambridge. The difference was that this was a paid site. Again, the note was pretty close to a form letter and an invitation to use IM. I had suspicions from the first note. I asked about whether he goes to the temple and if there was one close to him (knowing the answer but he obviously didn't) as well as whether he was sealed and how he felt about it. He replied he went frequently, didn't mention where, and said he enjoyed being sealed. The guy didn't have a clue what it all meant. I never received a response after asking where I fit in to the picture if he is already sealed.

Then there was quite a charismatic guy living in the Deep South: Louisiana to be specific. His profile stated all the right things, including temple recommend. He had wonderful ideas and ideals until I listened closer. Sweet guy suspected he'll be a bishop (I know of no other man who actually aspires to that thankless position). He needs a wife, obviously. The problem was he didn't see anything wrong with hanging out at the race track once in a while or placing a few bets. Okay; no one is perfect. His occasional glass of wine with his steak, or coffee to get through the day, struck a bad note. What I did know: I was new to the gospel and thought there was one standard for everyone. I suggested the Word of Wisdom was not really optional, especially if he went to the temple. No worry:

his best friend was the stake president. There was more but let us just say even LDS has men and women who are still children and push the proverbial envelope. Marry a guy like that and your companionship will likely end at the veil.

Multiple Marriages

I laughed when a friend, a divorced and remarried Roman Catholic considering joining us with his family, asked about LDS attitude toward divorce. I told him it happens and no one is happy about it but he won't be restricted from being an active member. What made me think of him is his commitment to God, and all the brothers and sisters in LDS who made a mistake within their lives, and have seen the error of their ways; be it in marriage or something else. There is however, a point where remarriage takes on even more significance, and while the second marriage is up for thought, the possible third and beyond can be critical.

Perhaps among the things for deliberation are:

Knowing if the prior spouses were similar in nature or physical resemblance to you.

Have you been courted because of it?

Does your prospective mate know where he or she went wrong or was it always the fault of their ex?

How long did they remain together?

You should always keep in mind when you get these answers whether it is always someone else's fault when something goes wrong? As we grow older we should have the wisdom to understand the frailties of our brethren and sisters, as well as our own. If the world were perfect we would not have to repent and there would have been no need for the atonement. Don't discount someone with multiple marriages simply because of the numbers: take the time to know them before making a decision.

You don't need to be a psychologist to discover what is important to the person you are dating. You have the advantage of lots of experience you didn't as a kid or young adult. You can find out how they feel about money by looking at how they dress, the vehicle they drive and how they shop for groceries. Is it in synch with a lifestyle you can adapt to? Do they like to go off fishing once in a while or sky dive? Are they involved in a business that takes a great deal of their time and you are not part of it? Don't anticipate things will change after you are married. What is ideal is that which both of you agree and understand from the beginning.

I remember living in Texas and dating a professional man before becoming a member. I had lots of clues that in spite of his being kind and gentle, he had problems. With three divorces behind him I was alert. He drove a beat-up old Ranger which could not build up enough speed to enter the highway when the light changed (you have to understand some of the Texas road systems for that explanation). He wouldn't buy a new vehicle because he was saving up for a trip to Europe and wanted to pay cash. It didn't matter that it might take an extra ten minutes to make it to the local small hospital Emergency Room when one of his patients was brought in.

Fred would not shop unless something was on sale. The final straw was when we went to a discount bookstore and he headed to the "deep" discount tables while I just browsed the regular sale items. He admonished me for spending more than needed there when another book would have been sufficient (my money by the way).

More recently another man was a wonderful guy, despite three previous marriages: two within the church. He and his last ex pretty much disagreed on everything. She earned more and it bothered him immensely. They very much led separate lives. He wanted a boat and used cars; protesting when she wanted new cars and enjoyed shopping for clothes. He prided himself on purchasing his clothes from thrift shops and online discount stores. These folks should never have been married in the first place. You might as well live alone than be alone within a marriage. He wed a strong woman and was looking for another. My friend knew enough to put the brakes on the relationship because it would only lead to being number four on his way to number five. He has not learned from his errors. In that situation, it is better to get out before the anguish turns to animus.

Of course we can't leave out the would-be writer. First, let me tell you I do whatever I can to encourage such individuals. I can write about things I know but have absolutely no creativity and marvel at those that do. His book, on the other hand, might just provoke wild laughter or deep sleep. The guy has been married three times and spent the last ten years writing a book on relationships. Duh. In his tome are 168 questions he believes should be asked of prospective mates. If the sheer number does not scare you off, the questions surely will. One of the first is whether or not they would sign a prenuptial agreement.

I have a theory on such matters. It should make little difference to you, but let me expound upon it anyway. My response to him said, in part, if one goes into a marriage with the fear or anticipation of ending it, the union is doomed. I understand how some who have been burned want to protect their assets: but each of his former spouses had signed such an agreement. I think he doomed it himself. Should not an eternal relationship be founded on love and trust? We're not youngsters. When you wed it should be because you can't live without him or her: not for material security.

The Superficial Things in Life

It's said that men are quite visual and statistics would bear that out; especially when it comes to profiles which get noticed and those that are bypassed. The problem is prevalent with both genders. Short of being morbidly obese, many people don't care what their partner looks like. If someone starts off describing themselves as beautiful, handsome, etc. instead of average, thin, or on the heavier side, it should be an instant clue to their personality. Humble is the hallmark of what we are supposed to be, isn't it? If you both think slim, tall, muscular, et al is important then you are a match. I'm amused at the obese guy who will settle for nothing less than cachectic, or the sister who is a bit chunky searching for cut and buff. Nothing is wrong with that as long as you both think the same way. If not, it's probably not going to work. Is it easier to love a guy with a full head of hair, or a woman who polishes her toenails? What is important to you?

The first thought of a stable individual looking for an eternal partner will be of their commitment to each other, the church, family, interests, and way down on the list physical attributes. Why would it matter if the guy is balding (and just so you know, that may be an indication of a genetically advanced hominid) or an inch or two shorter? Does it really matter if the woman wears red lipstick and high heels? Do you want a trophy or a spouse? Yes, everyone should be happy with their mate's appearance; but is that what will bring you to love?

Signing Up

Site fees range from about $8 per month if you take an extended membership of three to six months or longer. There are some which charge in the neighborhood of $15 to $35 for one month at a time. Not all sites are chock full of individuals in every age or interest range. You will have to find the one which suits you best but there are ways to get the most for your money. Find one of the sites and sign up for a limited (free) membership. You probably won't be able to send or receive messages but you will be able to browse and see if there are enough potential partners who meet your interests and wants. Wait for a week and see if anyone sends you a message. You will be able to look at their profile and decide if it's worth joining to see what they have to say. If it's a "flirt" they may not be a paid member either and you'll be wasting your time and dinero. If you decide to go for it, sign up for one month. Yes, it's more expensive but you'll know in a month whether the people you want to meet flock to this site, and you will not have wasted your money on an extended membership. Also, when the month is almost up delete your profile or give notice you are leaving: just about every site will offer you a deal to remain on the site at less than it would have cost you to extend it.

For certain, there are a lot more members on all the LDS matching services from Utah, Idaho, Nevada and the rest of the west; but that doesn't mean you won't find someone not too far from where you live. At our age, moving becomes a different issue than when we were younger. If you are free to relocate, don't limit your search to locals. Yes, it's a bit harder to date someone two thousand miles away: but you just may get to know them a lot better and faster through regular emails and phone conversations. You are also a step ahead of the younger men and women because you already know what you want in an eternal partner. Well, let me rephrase that: if you are divorced and learned from your mistakes, you will know what you want.

Remarriage: how long to wait?

There is no stock answer, although psychologists might have one. From a practical view and lots of observation, marrying on the rebound can doom any relationship from the start. Don't fall into a relationship just because you're lonely. Learn to live with yourself before you attempt to live with a spouse again. That applies to those of you who have lost a spouse too. Only you will know, but there are a few points to think about:

Don't marry someone exactly like your ex or deceased partner. If you're divorced, you will be repeating your initial error. If you are a widow/widower you will always be comparing your companion to their predecessor who will be remembered for all their kindness and love; not their human frailties.

If you are dwelling on what your ex did or said that brought about the arguments, wait. You are not ready to move on until you dump your baggage.

Singles Events

It would be remiss not to at least mention the Church sponsored singles events. You can make some interesting friends, although I'm not so convinced about finding an eternal partner, if you live in the mission field. However, this may not hold in the land of Zion where such events occur more frequently and are better attended. Here in the mission field we have a very high ratio of sisters to brothers, with an occasional non-member. It may come as a shock to those of you out west that there are places where stakes do not have any singles wards for adults. At least at singles events you can assume everyone is of like mind and move from there.

I have one more observation. The Word of Wisdom applies to more than chastity or what food and drink to reject. It also refers to eating in moderation. You may be a great person with a kind and loving soul who would make an ideal companion; but if you don't respect yourself enough to take care of the place the Holy Spirit dwells, then don't expect anyone else to. I'm not referring to chubby or a little overweight. Decent men and women don't look for eye candy: but they don't want to be embarrassed either. They'll never get to know how great you are if they don't come closer.

If you want to meet people at singles events, don't sit in a large group with all your friends: you already know them.

Dress appropriately. If you aren't sure, then ASK. I know it may be tough for guys but at a recent singles event held at a stake center, one guy came in shorts and flip-flop shoes, while another who was too large to sit on a regular pew seat, wore shorts as well. A few women wore jeans and the footwear appropriate for a beach. Everyone else wore Sunday meeting attire, as was requested on the flyers. Unless you are going to a beach event, you can be quite sure flip-flops are not appropriate. Wearing them in a church setting disrespects the sanctity of the meeting house and the people within it. It's a church event, people, show some respect.

A few months after taking the plunge, there was a 13 stake adult singles event in Connecticut. It included a boat ride down the Connecticut River, dinner, and speakers; some of whom were quite good. Unfortunately, it was like one large Relief Society meeting with a few men sprinkled in. The women were dressed well, for the most part. The few men there were dressed like they were prepared for a beach party, complete with floppy shoes. There were a few younger men who acted like teenagers and three men over 50: including Ron. His stake was also invited and he clung like scotch tape, smelling like a tobacco parlor. It was just as well since the other two men were creditable of remaining isolated. I asked Ron if he was still smoking and he admitted to it. I pressed him to become worthy so he could attend my endowment. I had the days numbered and could tell you at any time how long before I entered the sacred doors. He informed me the temple meant nothing to him, and the subject was dropped. So much for singles events and me.

You would think that with all the experience I gleaned in those early months of joining the church and diligently searching for an eternal partner I would have learned something. I guess I had to put it to paper before it sunk in.

Recently I had the opportunity to practice what I preached. Much against my better judgment I received a notice from one of the sites that I had something like seven messages. I forgot about the site until then. Curiosity got the best of me and I put down the eighteen dollars to join for one month. I figured it was worth a weekend of entertainment. A widower was bombarding me and I responded, since I didn't know who it was until I paid my fees. I told him I wasn't anxious to become involved with a widower but that made no impact. Then he brought up his home. The man described an old mobile home, falling apart with buckets necessary to catch the rain. Chuckie called it rural charm. I thought he was joking. He was not. I suggested it probably would not work since I hated camping, and call me a gold-digger for wanting to live in a home with insulation and a roof. He pretty much called me materialistic for wanting such luxuries. So be it.

So, what is the point? Marry because he or she has walked away with your heart; not because someone else thinks they are a "good catch". If it does not happen here, it will across the veil. Do not rush it, and better yet, be very sure you are marrying for love; not just to fulfill a requirement or bucket list. It is your life now: not that of your children. Be firm but be careful. Know that the Lord loves you and sometimes we are permitted to err, in order to make mistakes.

Just be happy it is not you that fell into the trap.

Wrapping it All Up

I know there are a lot of folks who think anyone who treats their dogs or cats with love and compassion are misguided. I disagree and actually do not care what others believe. My pets have never lied to me, are totally forgiving, and love unconditionally. As such, Drummer is a big part of this 3 ring circus called my life. Let me just take a few minutes why.

After meeting Ron, I decided that living might not be so bad and began to come to grips with losing my beloved cat Maxx, I decided to live again, and share my life with a dog. I knew it would be a retriever, although a black one would remind me too much of my first dog, Charlie. It couldn't be one that was too large for me to handle, since a foot-drop after a stroke years before, made my walking less stable.

My decision matrix was not complicated. It had to be a shelter dog, male, around two years old. I searched online for all the shelter dogs in a two hundred-fifty mile radius, and drove to visit shelters from the Pennsylvania border to the middle of Connecticut.

I found what seemed like an ideal match and sent Ron to see the pooch in the Sheffield shelter, a few miles away. He told me he started the adoption procedure and if I didn't take the pooch, he would: as a companion for his aging Golden Lab. That

Friday afternoon we arrived at the Sheffield, Vermont shelter to find a very friendly yellow retriever/pit bull. He was so excited his tail thumped like a drummer. It was the right time of year and appropriate to name him Drummer Boy.

The poor little guy had scars all over his face, and later I found the rest of his body was not unscathed either. The dog's snout had been damaged and his breathing appeared to be impaired, also with a loud whistle. He had been seen by a vet but they could not determine the cause. He had obviously been the loser in more than one dog fight and abused. It made sense after learning his history. Although little is actually known, over the last few year the pieces of the puzzle have fallen into place.

He was picked up as a stray in Virginia and brought to a kill shelter. As fate would have it, a kind Samaritan from Vermont, routinely takes trips down there and rescues animals that have potential as companions. They are spayed or neutered and placed in foster homes for a few weeks. The pets are brought up to Vermont shelters for adoption (which tells us Vermont residents are more responsible than many other places since their shelters are not burgeoning with discarded creatures).

All was fine until it was time to get in the car. Prince (the Golden Lab) got in the SUV first. Drummer cried, peed, and resisted. He trembled, whined, peed and pooped all over the new pet bedding, on the way to New Hampshire.

Once we arrived and got into the house, he was playful, inquisitive and went upstairs where he found a bed he adopted. Within an hour he settled in and was playing with Prince. Bob went out the front door to get the mail and Drummer watched. He also noticed the storm door was not latched and headed for daylight. At the shelter they named him Ross. I doubt he knew that name or the one I had given him that day. So, calling him was sort of useless. He ran around the property, checked out the neighbors, and then walked back up the steps.

We did notice a few other signs of abuse. He was skittish when feet moved, had no idea what a treat or dog biscuit was, and apparently never had a toy.

It took several weeks to introduce Drummer to the SUV, and after a while it was no struggle. But, what it definitely told me was that his previous experiences with transportation were terrifying.

I also took some training. When he lifted his leg on a chair I yelled at him. The pitiful animal cowered in fear and waited to be struck: and lost control of his bladder. You'd think I would learn, wouldn't you? A few weeks later he emptied a trash bag and I sternly asked if he did it. He was so scared he peed. I learned.

For the first six months, Drummer would run into my bedroom whenever someone came into the house: including my brother and sister-in-law. The worst problem we faced was when my mother came into my room. He would be friendly to her anywhere else in the house; but in the bedroom he would growl. I would sternly tell him to stop and he did for each incident. We used a few other techniques to get him comfortable with her, as recommended by the vet. However, when I wasn't home, the door had to be closed. He was so fearful he would growl and snarl if she approached the closed door. Eventually what we call liverwurst therapy (he loves the stuff and if he wants it he can only get it from her) worked wonders and the problem ceased.

Another manifestation of his abuse comes with his nightmares. I'm not talking about the dreams where dogs run and bark in their sleep. He cried with abject terror and had to wake him up. It happens rarely these days but the memory remains. He was a dog who would not bark, but rather would hide in our room. It was close to a year before he would bark at someone or some animal outside. Yet, if he is outside and wants to come in, he will sit and wait without so much as a whimper.

I've learned much about his history. The papers said he was a stray and about ten months old: not two years. But, the dog is incredibly smart; I doubt he was an abandoned stray. We traveled across the country to Utah, usually making pit stops at rest areas with well kept pet areas. One particular time he was getting antsy and I pulled into a truck rest area. There were tall weeds, noisy diesels, and it was otherwise barren. Drummer did his thing and stood still, tail dropped, absolutely forlorn, staring at me. I called him and asked what's wrong. He came running over, jumped on me and was unquestionably overjoyed. I think he had been abandoned in an area like that or it was the kind of place he was taken to fight.

I think people who insist on pedigrees, papers, and prestige are denying themselves the joys of enriching their own lives as well as the sense of saving the life of one of God's beloved creatures.

While writing this little tome, my loyal companion succumbed to cancer. It was a reminder that we do not avoid pain when we come to the Lord. End of mortality is part of the process. The hard part is the void. But it also makes me wonder why our pets have to endure and suffer trials too. He came from a shelter and it was quite evident by his physical and mental scars, that he was abused. I don't have the answers. But, I know that when we stand before the bar, there will be no excuses for inhumanity.

The other thought regarding my grief, is that too often people blame the Lord. I know a sister who is angry at God because her family is being torn apart by circumstances she has not been able to control. Whose fault (and it is not the Lord) is irrelevant. Her prayers were not answered so she has given up and placed the blame squarely where it does not belong.

Other Stuff

I don't know where William is; and frankly do not care.

I served our local mission for over 3 years as the mission medical specialist. I'm told we had one of the lowest medical costs in the country during that period. Yet I was not, and did not know, I was supposed to have been set apart. I think back to that and it does not matter if no one bothered to tell me: I did my job, served the Lord and know He is keeping track even if His servants are not.

During the 3rd year of that activity, I was called to be a service missionary for the Pathway program. It was a blessing for me, as well as the students. My companion, a widowed brother (who has escaped to Happy Valley in retirement), taught the BOM the first year; I did it the second. Many of those individuals still keep in contact. It has been joyful to watch how so many have grown in the gospel as well as expanded their vistas.

My current calling is teaching Gospel Doctrine. My classes are rather tame, compared to those in the west: but we learn and laugh an awful lot ☺. Come and join us!

Meet the Author

Corie is a retired physician assistant who also worked in non-clinical administrative positions in the business of medicine. She has been a contributor to Deseret News, Family How, and Deseret Connect. In addition to authoring a humorous book on the foibles of life as well as one on building your own home, she is a professional writer whose work can be found online and in print. Corie is proud to have done service projects for the Salvation Army, Medical Reserve Corps, and other volunteer organizations.

Contact her at: soaringsaint@gmail.com